REFRAMING
FOSTER CARE

REFRAMING FOSTER CARE

FILTERING YOUR FOSTER PARENTING JOURNEY THROUGH THE LENS OF THE GOSPEL

JASON JOHNSON

credo
house publishers

> **This resource is dedicated to those who are giving all so that a child can gain much. Thank you for doing what you're doing. It matters, and it's worth it.**

WE LOVE BECAUSE HE FIRST LOVED US.

1 John 4:19

CONTENTS

INTRODUCTION

A Quick Note . . . 1

Why, What, and How? Three Things to Know about this Resource 5

Who Is this Book for? 11

The Gospel in Foster Care 13

1. *Foster Care, Adoption, and Saying Yes to the Unknown* 21

2. *Faithfulness, Foster Care, and Trusting God with the Rest* 31

3. *An Invitation into an Entirely New Story* 43

4. *Counting the Costs of Fostering or Adopting* 53

5. *Foster Care Is Spiritual Warfare* 67
Story 77

6. *Reframing Your Season
of Struggle* 83

7. *Redefining Success and Failure
as a Foster Parent* 93

8. *Loving Out of
Our Poverty* 105

9. *Busyness, Obedience, and the
Perfect Time to Foster or Adopt* 113

10. *The Best Thing You Can Do
for Your Marriage* 125

11. *Foster Care and What I Feared Most for My Own Kids* 137
Story 146

12. *For the Husband
Who Isn't Sure* 151

13. *Loving a Child
Who Might Leave* 161

14. *The Sovereignty of God in Foster Care* 171

15. *Foster Care: A Family-Giving Mechanism* 179
Story 186

16. *How Foster Care Preaches the Gospel and Why We Must Let It* 191

17. *Rehumanizing Foster Care* 203

18. *The Other Side of Foster Care* 213
Story 224

19. *Crucifying the Hero Complex* 229

20. *Diversity, Guilt, and Battling the Enemy of Comparison* 237

About the Author 253

A QUICK NOTE...

We became a foster family in 2012. Our first placement arrived at our home just a few weeks after our having finalized all our training hours, inspections, and paperwork. It was a Wednesday, around 7:30 p.m. Our lives forever changed that night. We knew then that nothing would ever be the same again, but even more than that, we knew then that nothing *could ever be the same.*

We know things now that we can never unknow, have seen things that we can never unsee, heard things that we can never unhear, and felt things that we can never unfeel. Nothing will ever again be the same. Nothing can.

Our journey, in part, has been documented through a collection of blogs over these years—accounts and recollections that have been sorted through, condensed, reformatted, and turned into the chapters of this book. They are reflections on some really wonderful and beautiful things, and some really hard and ugly things—because foster care is nothing if not an intricate collection of some really extraordinary along with some extremely difficult experiences. Through it all we have changed as individuals, as husband and wife and as mom and dad. Our daughters have changed. Our family has changed. Our faith has changed, and our understanding of God's capacity to turn some really broken things into some really beautiful things has deepened in ways we could never have anticipated.

That's what this book is about—the gospel—God's capacity to bring great beauty out of tragic brokenness. That's who this book is for—those needing to see the beauty of what they are doing, not *in spite* of the brokenness that surrounds it but *through* it. This isn't a rose-colored-lens look at foster care or a glossing over of the very real and hard fallout that comes with stepping into systemically broken places. It's an honest recognition of the hard with a push in the direction of "reframing" how we see and feel and understand some of the situation's bigger and more beautiful ramifications and aspects.

We hope *ReFraming Foster Care* can be an encouragement to you, whether you read it alone or journey through it with a small group. We pray that the gospel, God's capacity to bring great beauty out of tragic brokenness, will be made rich and vibrant and evident to you through these pages and will ultimately sustain you in the good work you're doing on behalf of the kids and families you're loving.

Thank you for doing what you're doing. We're honored to be on this journey with you.

Jason, Emily, and the Girls

WHY, WHAT, AND HOW

Three things to know about this resource:

1. WHY

It's essential that everything about foster care—all the unique experiences, emotions, and situations you'll find yourself walking through during this journey—be filtered through the lens of God's truths found in the gospel—not only as the end to which all of this points but also as the means by which you can be sustained, encouraged, and motivated to continue on in a healthy way. *ReFraming Foster Care* is designed to do just that.

2. WHAT

ReFraming Foster Care is a collection of writings chronicling our own personal fostering journey, sharing some of the good and the bad, the beautiful and the broken, and many of the most impactful experiences we have encountered along the way. Each section contains a short reading followed by a series of "Personal Reflection" and "Group Discussion" questions, as well as a "Plan of Action" section to help you take the necessary next steps forward in your journey. You will also find inspirational stories from real life foster families sharing pieces of their own fostering journey.

This book can be used as a personal devotional and/or small group discussion guide. It's designed to be short, quick, and easy to work through, with no outside work needing to be done. The goal of *ReFraming Foster Care* is to help you filter the unique experiences and emotions you'll encournter in foster care through the lens of the gospel so that you can find the comfort, perspective, and refreshment you need.

3. HOW

The format of this book is intended to be simple and light, not burdensome with too much demanding material or a disciplined agenda to work through. It can be used in a variety of ways:

CLASSIC BOOK STYLE

Find your favorite chair at home or in the corner of your local coffee shop and get comfortable. You can read *ReFraming Foster Care* just as you would any other book, from one chapter to the next. While the material doesn't necessarily have to be read in sequential order— each chapter tends to stand on its own—you can certainly read it through from cover to cover.

PERSONAL DEVOTIONAL

Maybe you need more than just a leisurely read—something that engages you a little more deeply and pushes you a little further. *ReFraming Foster Care* can be used as a personal devotional as well. Simply carve out five, ten, or fifteen minutes to read through a short chapter and respond to the prompts and questions given. Glean from each section what you need and then go about your day, remembering and reflecting upon how the Scripture or principles helped frame your journey for the day.

SMALL GROUP SETTING

Whether it's in your weekly small group from church, a foster parent support group, or just a group of friends getting together regularly to encourage one another, you can use *ReFraming Foster Care* as a group discussion guide as well. Simply approach each chapter as a discussion stimulus and utilize the suggested discussion questions to help move the conversation forward. You may choose as many sections to cover in a group setting as you'd like, or simply focus on the one most needed for the group at the given time. The questions are intended to promote discussion but not to be exhaustive—feel free to use some of them, all of them, or none of them—and always be thinking of others that would be helpful to ask and discuss.

A few considerations if you are using *ReFraming Foster Care* in a group setting:

1. NO LEADER NECESSARY

My hope is that this book is as accessible and user-friendly as possible so that any group can pick it up and use it, whether or not there is a designated "leader." The material is written so that members of the group can share responsibilities for reading and helping others navigate through different sections.

2. STRUCTURE OF SESSIONS

The structure of this resource is fluid—designed for new participants to join in or leave the group at any point. The chapters, as I've indicated, don't build on one another and aren't necessarily intended to be read sequentially. Groups can begin with any chapter and choose to move on to another at any point, given the particular needs and dynamics of those in the group.

3. A DISCUSSION STARTER

The goal of each section is to promote discussion. This resource isn't written as an in-depth study but is designed to promote in-depth thought and conversation. Each chapter covers a unique perspective on a particular aspect of fostering that may challenge you to think about the topic differently from the way you have before. The goal isn't for you to agree with everything presented in this book. Rather, it's for everything presented in this book to act as a catalyst for healthy and encouraging group discussion.

4. GUIDELINES

Your group, whatever its format, needs to be a safe place to learn, share, and be vulnerable with one another. Many of the topics discussed will draw out deep emotional responses and raw feelings—all of which require a healthy environment in order to be processed. In that light, here are a few suggested ground rules designed to help make your group experience positive and encouraging for everyone:

- Commit to confidentiality. What's shared in this group stays in this group.
- Refrain from offering unsolicited advice. Assume the role of encourager; coach only when requested.
- Use "I" statements rather than "you" or "we" statements. The objective is for all participants to be personally vulnerable and encouraged, not to make generalizations.
- Leave room for everyone to speak. Allow all to participate . . . but no one to dominate.
- Avoid trying to give the "right" answers; focus more on giving "honest" answers. Transparency will make your time richer and more effective.

WHO IS THIS BOOK FOR?

ReFraming Foster Care is written for current foster parents, prospective foster parents, and those simply wanting to learn how to relate to and support those who are engaged in fostering.

Whether single or married, fostering with the hope of adopting, or fostering as an end in itself, foster parents face a unique set of circumstances and experience a range of emotions to which few outside the foster care community can fully relate.

It's critical for foster parents to access a well of encouragement from which they can make sense of their experiences, as well as an understanding community with which they can connect, into which they can lean, and from which they can draw support. It's also essential that they have a place to freely share the joys and struggles of fostering, as well as a safe environment in which to process the raw and difficult emotions they experience in a healthy way. This book is designed to help cultivate that for you.

The goal of *ReFraming Foster Care* is to equip, support, encourage, and sustain you in the gospel—no matter where you are on your fostering journey.

The book is meant to be an encouraging reminder that your work is worth it and that you're not alone.

THE GOSPEL IN FOSTER CARE

The Gospel is our "WHY"

The work of Jesus on our behalf compels us in turn to work on behalf of others. Why would we step into the hard? Lean into the broken? Open up our families to be vulnerable to the traumatic and difficult? Because that's what Jesus has done for us. We lay down our lives for others because He first laid down His for us—perfectly, sacrificially, and sufficiently.

> *By this we know love, that he laid down his life for us, and we ought to lay down our lives for the brothers. . . . Little children, let us not love in word or talk but in deed and in truth.*
>
> 1 John 3:16,18

Christ saw our brokenness and embraced us in our weakness, adopted us into His family, and changed the course of our lives forever.

This beautiful picture of the gospel, and its vivid implications for our care of the most vulnerable, plays itself out through two primary aspects of theology:

- **The Doctrine of Our Adoption**
- **The Doctrine of His Incarnation**

These two pillar doctrines form the strong and sturdy foundation of our "why."

THE DOCTRINE OF OUR ADOPTION

One of the prominent images running throughout Scripture, depicting the character of God and His work on our behalf, is the picture of family. Specifically, the illustration is rooted in the relationship between God as our Father and ourselves as His dearly loved children.

> *See what kind of love the Father has given to us, that we should be called children of God; and so we are.*
>
> 1 John 3:1

The hinge upon which this new relationship with God depends is beautifully illustrated in Scripture through the New Testament repetition of the word "adoption." Consider the following passages:

> *He predestined us for adoption to himself as sons through Jesus Christ, according to the purpose of his will.*
>
> Ephesians 1:5

> *For you did not receive the spirit of slavery to fall back into fear, but you have received the Spirit of adoption as sons, by whom we cry, "Abba! Father!"*
>
> Romans 8:15

We were once outside the family of God, but now, through the work of Christ on our behalf, we have been adopted as dearly loved sons and daughters. We experience the rights and privileges of being known and loved as His very own!

A new identity is born from a new way of relating to God—as our Father—and of His relating to us—as His children.

If our adoption into God's family is at the core of the gospel, then the gospel is certainly at the core of our calling to care for vulnerable kids in our world who need loving, safe, and permanent families to call their own.

WE CARE FOR THE VULNERABLE BECAUSE WE HAVE BEEN GREATLY CARED FOR BY JESUS.

The theology of our adoption helps form the basis of our "why." Why would we care for vulnerable children by welcoming them into our families? Because that's what Christ has done for us.

THE DOCTRINE OF HIS INCARNATION

The word *incarnation* literally means "assuming human form." The doctrine of Christ's incarnation speaks of God stepping into humanity, wrapping Himself in flesh, and living completely and fully as both God and man. This wonder is most notably recognized at Christmas with the birth of Jesus, yet its implications are far more pervasive.

All this took place to fulfill what the Lord had spoken by the prophet: "Behold, the virgin shall conceive and bear a son, and they shall call his name Immanuel" (which means, God with us).

Matthew 1:22–23

The incarnation reveals much about who God is and what God does. It tells us that He is the kind of God who sees broken and hard things and doesn't step *away* from them, but steps *into* them. He is Immanuel, God "with us." He wrapped Himself up in our brokenness, carried our brokenness to the cross, and was broken by our brokenness so that we don't have to be broken anymore. God saw us in our plight and moved toward us, not away from us. In essence He says, "I see you where you are and I'm coming after you!" That's the gospel.

The apostle Paul reiterates the story of the incarnation of Christ and beautifully ties it in to God's redemptive pursuit of humanity to make us His children, writing,

> *When the fullness of time had come, God sent forth his Son, born of woman, born under the law, to redeem those who were under the law, so that we might receive adoption as sons.*
>
> Galatians 4:4–5

Jesus was "born of woman" (incarnated) in order "that we might receive adoption" into His family.

If the incarnation of Jesus is at the core of the gospel, our stepping toward the hard and broken is certainly at the core of our calling to care for vulnerable kids.

The theology of Christ's incarnation helps form the basis of our "why." Why would we immerse—in a sense *incarnate*—ourselves into these hard and broken places? Because that's what Christ has done for us.

The implications of the doctrine of the incarnation are broad. The opportunities for each unique individual to "incarnate" themselves into hard and broken places are endless and infinitely creative.

This moves the conversation beyond the parameters of foster care, adoption, or orphan care in some other capacity—although each of these provides a ready outlet through which Christians can respond (perhaps that's why James 1:27 describes leaning into the lives of the vulnerable as one of the purest and most undefiled reflections of the gospel). Incarnation, however, goes further, speaking to a renewed posture and perspective toward the world around us in all matters of justice, mercy, and sacrifice. One where we see hard places and broken people and say, "I see you where you are and I'm coming after you."

THE BEGINNING, MIDDLE, AND END

At the core of our motivation to care for the vulnerable is the heart of God demonstrated through the gospel on our behalf. It's the gospel—the story of Christ stepping into our brokenness (incarnation) and drawing us into the security and assurance of His provision and protection (adoption)—that acts as the guide not only to *why* but also to *how* we must care for the vulnerable.

THREE THINGS THE GOSPEL DOES:

1. It compels us into it.

The work of Jesus on our behalf becomes the primary motivation for us to work on others' behalf: He said to us, "I see you where you are and I'm coming after you!" We echo that same sentiment into the lives of those around us. The gospel changes the questions we ask, from "Why would we do hard things for others?" to "In light of what Jesus did for us, why would we NOT do hard things?"

2. It sustains us in the midst of it.

When the work of foster care gets especially difficult—when we're left asking "Why are we doing this?"—the gospel reminds us that the work is worth it; it infuses meaning into the struggle and context into the difficulty.

3. It manifests itself through it.

Caring for the vulnerable is one of the purest and most undefiled demonstrations of the gospel the world will ever see (James 1:27). The echoes of the gospel in foster care are beautiful and vivid.

The gospel compels us into foster care, sustains us when the journey gets difficult, and is precisely what we want put on display through it; our response to Christ's "good news" serves as an irrefutable demonstration of the willingness of Jesus to step *toward* hard places and broken people and points to His capacity to bring great beauty out of it all.

The gospel is our most compelling "WHY."

The gospel compelling us into foster care doesn't guarantee that everything will be easy, but it does give meaning to the struggles and an assurance that while ours is anything but a simple journey, it is a worthy one. It provides hope in the midst of uncertainties and perspective within the seemingly incomprehensible confusion, frustration, and exhaustion that will come our way. The gospel is nothing if not the capacity of Jesus to bring breathtaking beauty out of tragic brokenness.

This is the gospel in foster care, and it's what we have in mind when we use the word "gospel" throughout the pages of this book. It's central to everything we believe is necessary for us to "do" foster care well.

You may not have stepped into foster care with an explicit motivation to serve Jesus, . . . or perhaps that's been your impetus all along. You may not have gotten involved in order to lay down your life for kids the way Jesus did for you, . . . or perhaps that has been your posture from the very beginning. You may not have determined to put the gospel on display as your end goal, . . . or perhaps that has always been your hope. Wherever you're coming from and whatever it is that brought you to where you are now, the truth for you is this: *here you are*. It doesn't matter what brought you into it—you're in it now, and it's important that you be connected with others, supported, encouraged, and cared for.

That's the heart of this book.

CHAPTER 1

FOSTER CARE, ADOPTION, AND SAYING YES TO THE UNKNOWN

We recently found one of our daughters crying in bed. She had seemed fine the last we had seen her before going upstairs, so this took us a bit off guard. In a home with four daughters there always seems to be something to cry about, but when she calmed down enough to share with us what it was this time, we were shocked.

Hitler.

That's right, HITLER was on her mind, and apparently had been for the past several weeks. *What?!* She told us that her class was doing a research project at school and that each student could select any topic they wanted to learn more about. She didn't choose butterflies or dolphins or dandelions or the North Pole. She chose, of all possible topics, Hitler, and had been haunted by the things she has learned ever since—justifiably so—and afraid that bad things like that might happen to her—understandably so. "My mind can't stop thinking about it," she confessed. Having carried this burden alone for so long, she finally broke that night in bed.

Is she one day going to learn about these horrific events of the past? Yes, this detail will inevitably become a part of her education. Should she? Probably—it's important for her to understand that part of our history. But not right now. Not yet. No nine-year-old can comprehend these things. No nine-year-old should have to. (We arranged to have the research topic changed!)

The mercy of not knowing

There's danger in knowing things before such knowledge is necessary, appropriate, or helpful. It can be too much too soon. This is true in the "big" things of life but also in the daily, mundane, routine ones. I don't want those gruesome images haunting my nine-year-old for the same reasons I don't want my four-year-old to know how to open a childproof bottle of medicine. She isn't ready to carry the weight of that information. It could be detrimental, not useful. Harmful rather than helpful.

We see God making the same kinds of assessments in Scripture. He called Abraham to leave his fairly settled and comfortable life to journey toward a new land with which he was wholly unfamiliar. In Genesis 12:1, 4 God says to him, "*Go from your country and your kindred and your father's house to the land that I will show you. . . . So Abram went, as the LORD had told him.*"

He left the certainty of his homeland for the uncertainty of what God hadn't yet shown him. Not because it was the easiest thing to do, but because God had called him to do it and promised that it would be worth it in the end. Hebrews 11:8 summarizes long after the fact: "*By faith Abraham obeyed when he was called to go out to a place that he was to receive and an inheritance. And he went out, not knowing where he was going.*" Abraham had no idea how significant the hard things or how plentiful the good things would be along the journey. All he knew was that God wanted him to go, . . . and so he did. The rest of the information unfolded, as needed, along the way.

God will intentionally, lovingly, and mercifully refrain from providing us with certain pieces of information at certain times along our journeys—not to deprive us of knowing things but to protect us from the burden of knowing too much too soon—a seemingly subtle distinction with significantly different implications. This mercy of not knowing, in fact, is one of His most profound acts of mercy toward us. He says go, we ask where, and He simply encourages us to not worry about that right now.

A whole lot of hope

There are very few things about the foster care and adoption journey my wife and I knew before stepping into it. We knew there was a huge problem in our city, that vulnerable kids needed loving homes, and that God was leading us to get involved. But that was about it. We knew what we needed to know at the time, and it was enough to allow us to step into something largely unknown. It was frustrating and intimidating at times—not knowing what we didn't know— but perhaps knowing more would have been even more frightening.

If you had asked me five years ago to tell you what I thought fostering and adopting would be like, there could have been no way for me to have anticipated with any accuracy what was to come. The experience has ebbed and flowed in intensity, and evolved our family through multiple iterations, scenarios, and compositions—driven by what seems to have been a constant reality of chaos punctuated by moments of calm. It has been a collection of experiences and emotions for which we could never have fully prepared, some ending in beautiful ways with others continuing to linger in broken ways. We've discovered that there really is no conclusion to any of this—this endless succession of good and bad, beautiful and broken—that these experiences and their lasting implications will remain a forever ongoing part of what and who we are. In many ways the most impactful aspects of foster care and adoption today were at one point the most hidden and least expected. We were simply unaware and mercifully incapable of comprehending all that was to come. Mercy.

The mercy of God spared us from the burden of carrying information that would have potentially paralyzed us; He simply invited us on a journey: He said go, we asked where, He said don't worry about that right now, and we said — with a little bit of fear and a whole lot of hope: "Okay, let's do it.

All the good and the bad, the easy and the hard

Foster care and adoption have turned our family into something it would never have been able to become on its own. The good has far exceeded anything we could have hoped would come from this endeavor, permeating places in our home and hearts of which we had been largely unaware. Five years earlier, if God had told us how good this whole thing would be, we likely wouldn't have believed Him. But He didn't do that, and for that we're grateful.

At the same time, foster care and adoption have required our family to grieve and struggle under the weight of hard things we would ordinarily have gone to great lengths to avoid. The experience has been far more difficult than we could ever have anticipated, pressing us down into the cracks and crevices of other people's broken stories, while exposing the deep flaws in our own. Five years ago, if God had told us how hard this thing would be, we likely wouldn't have moved forward in obedience. But He didn't do that, and for that we are grateful.

We've seen a little girl placed in our home on a permanent basis, becoming a crucial part of our new forever family. We've wept through the heartache of having to say goodbye to another we also loved as our own—despite her begging us to let her stay, we had absolutely no control over the situation. We've struggled through the seemingly insurmountable hurdles of fostering a teenage mom on the brink of aging out—a baby struggling to raise her own baby with a lifetime of past trauma rearing its ugly head in every aspect of her present reality. We've invited another young mom, and her newborn twins, into our home in order to prevent foster care from becoming a part of their precious, brand new, and completely innocent stories—a clash of worlds under one roof, with uniquely beautiful and unbelievably difficult outcomes born as a result.

In the end, it's the mercy of God that He doesn't show us everything that will unfold in the foster care and adoption journey the moment we first say yes to it. All the hard would be too unbearable and all the good would be too unbelievable.

A hope that outpaces

Whether you're just now considering leaving your land of certainty to set foot into the vast unknowns of foster care or adoption or are immersed in the journey already but uncertain how this whole thing is going to play out, let your faith in what you *do* know drive you. Never let your fear of what you don't know deter you. I'm convinced that God is far more pleased by your willingness to be faithful on the journey than He is concerned about your inability to control any of the good or bad that will inevitably come along the way.

So let's allow our hope in what's to come outpace all the uncertainties of what it will take to actually get there. It will be far more difficult than you could possibly imagine, . . . and far more beautiful than you could ever have hoped for.

" It's the mercy of God that He doesn't show us everything that will unfold in the foster care and adoption journey the moment we first say yes to it. All the hard would be too unbearable and all the good would be too unbelievable.

PERSONAL REFLECTION

1. How has foster care been more difficult than you thought it would be? How has it been more beautiful and rewarding?

2. What one aspect of the experience, had you known up front how hard it would be, would have made it more difficult for you to say yes to foster care? After the fact, what have you learned through it? In hindsight, how has God been merciful in the "not knowing"?

3. What one thing, had you known ahead of time how amazing it would be, would you have had a hard time believing? What has been one of the most surprising highlights of the fostering journey for you? How has God demonstrated His mercy through this experience?

GROUP DISCUSSION

1. What truth, idea, or "aha!" has stood out for you most clearly in this session? Why?

2. In what other areas of your life has God "intentionally, lovingly, and mercifully refrained from providing you with certain pieces of information" to protect you from the burden of knowing them too soon?

3. What have been the most difficult aspects of fostering for you? The most beautiful? Have either of these surprised you? What have you learned about yourself, the world, God, and the gospel through these experiences?

4.   What are one or two primary ways in which you have experienced the "mercy of not knowing" in your foster care journey?

PLAN OF ACTION

1.   What specific perspectives, attitudes, or ways of thinking might need to change in order for you to more effectively live out the ideas discussed in this section?

2.   What specific actions or behaviors might need to change in order for you to more completely live out the ideas discussed in this section?

3.   Based on what has been discussed in this section, complete the following statement as thoroughly and honestly as you can: *I will choose to honor God through this experience by . . .*

God does not require us to carry the whole at once.
He mercifully unties the bundle, and gives us first one stick,
which we are to carry today, and then another,
which we are to carry tomorrow, and so on.

JOHN NEWTON

CHAPTER 2

FAITHFULNESS, FOSTER CARE, AND TRUSTING GOD WITH THE REST

I travel often for work. Enough that the whole experience is fairly routine for me. Airports, car rentals, hotel rooms, and even long security lines and flight delays—I'm fairly numb to it all by now. It's just a means to the end of getting where I need to go.

However, a recent trip to Chicago was anything but routine. My oldest daughter came along with me, changing the entire dynamic.

In the months leading up to the trip she devoured at least a dozen books about Chicago's history. She researched museums, parks, and famous sites she hoped to see and visit. She wanted to know as much about the city as she could so she could get the most possible out of her time there. It was a great trip, but oddly enough what I'll remember most about our time together has nothing to do with actually being *in* Chicago. It has everything to do with the journey of our getting there.

It began with her fascination over the x-ray machine that scanned our bags, moving quickly to her curiousity as to why everyone else at our gate was also going to Chicago; her wide-eyed wonder as she felt the thrust of the plane and watched the wheels leaving the runway as we headed for the sky; her intrigue as we leveled off five miles above the earth (while snapping pictures from every conceivable angle through the small window next to her); her awe at the shops and cafes and restaurants in the massive Chicago airport—"like a city inside a building", she said; her irrepressible smiles as we rode the train to pick up our car; and her complete loss for words as we neared the Chicago skyline just as the sun was setting, she again taking pictures, only stopping long enough to ensure that I too was taking in everything she was seeing, like a corroborating witness testifying that all of this was really happening. These are the things I will remember— watching my baby girl's eyes light up at all the things she was experiencing on our way to where it was we were going. In those moments it had nothing to do with arriving at the destination and everything to do with enjoying the journey.

A scale of outcomes

On that day what had become ordinary to me was a pure joy to her. My routine was her delight. Sure, she was looking forward to our destination, but not at the expense of appreciating as much of the journey as she could. I needed to see—to be reminded of—that reality in more ways than one. Maybe you do too.

We live in a results-driven society, one that measures success and worth on a scale of outcomes, accomplishments, and achievements. It's all about the destination and what we can produce en route. In some ways this is good—driving us to pursue excellence and bring about new and better outcomes; yet in many ways it's dangerous—forcing us to be so focused on where we think we need to be that we lose sight of where we actually are and of all the beauty and wonder and opportunity surrounding us.

Faithful servant

We wanted to "fix" our foster daughter. I knew we couldn't, but we wanted to undo in a matter of months what had been ingrained within her over the course of seventeen years. In an idealistic sense we wanted her to "be" better and "do" better at life, for her own sake and for that of her baby boy—but in all honesty, partly for our sake as well. It's as though somehow, at least in our minds, her progress worked to validate us as foster parents, to justify our decision to do this and assure those around us that we do in fact know what we're doing (at least sometimes!). We wanted her to succeed, and we wanted *us* to succeed as well, and there's nothing inherently wrong with that desire. It's just that for us as foster parents it's easy to measure our "success" by the wrong standards and to try to find validation in the wrong places.

While her story is far from over, it has been one in which every worst-possible-case outcome has materialized. Shortly before her eighteenth birthday she decided to run away, packing as many clothes and baby supplies as a few duffle bags would allow; when we turned around they were gone. It had been a heated night, the culmination of weeks of intense conversations, standoffs, and a thick wall of resistance she had been constructing between us and herself for some time. She has lived in chaos for two-thirds of her life. It's what she knows and where she's comfortable. Our home wasn't about disaray and turmoil, and she'd had enough. She needed out, and it didn't matter where to—the not knowing aspect was familiar to and comfortable for her; in many ways the uncertainty was more of a home to her than the stability of our house had ever been.

After phone calls to our agency and case workers and, per their instruction, to the police, we ended the night with two officers in our living room asking what she had been wearing, if we had any idea where she might have gone, and whether we felt as though her son—or she herself—were in danger. Questions for which we had very few answers. Our young daughters sat on the couch and watched solemnly as everything we had fought so hard to prevent was now happening, at eleven o'clock, on a school night, in our living room.

Not long afterward I received a text from my dad, whom I'd been updating throughout the ordeal, that initially threw me off:

"Does this feel like defeat to you?"

Not great timing, Dad. Perhaps it's a little too early to be asking questions like that! That's what I wanted to type back. However, the more I considered the question the more I appreciated it. It forced me to confront something that moment and dig deeply to find the right answer to a question that, left to its own timing, would inevitably haunt me.

This whole situation *wanted* to feel like defeat; it wanted me to believe that we had failed. It wanted me to answer an emphatic yes to him—yes, it does feel like defeat, like failure, like it's all been in vain, and I wonder whether it really was worth it. That's how I wanted to respond, but I knew I couldn't. I knew there had to be more to it than that. While the struggle of that evening was still raw in my mind and heart, his question forced me to rise above it, to grasp the bigger picture and to take rest in the truth of a story God was playing out that was much bigger than just this night.

> *"I try to think that success is doing it in the first place, not necessarily any outcomes we can produce. At least that's what helps me sleep at night."*

That was my answer. I forced my fingers to type each individual letter, not to impress him with my words but to impress upon my heart the importance of my believing those words—each and every one of them. His text was a gift to me that night, forcing me to fall asleep believing what is true about the journey, the destination, and the faithfulness of God through it all.

I'm convinced God is more pleased by our willingness to be faithful along the journey of foster care than He is concerned about our ability to achieve a certain outcome through it. *"Well done, good and *successful* servant?"* No. *"Well done, good and FAITHFUL servant."* Faithfulness—not achieving some outcome that only God has the capacity to produce—constitutes our "success." Of course we want to see measures of health and stability, progress and hope in the lives of these kids from hard places. But what happens if she doesn't graduate, doesn't get a job, doesn't break free from those destructive patterns of behavior and thinking? What happens if our definition of "success" never materializes in her life? Honestly, I don't know. Does that mean we have failed her? Does that mean our work on her behalf has been in vain? Was the journey along the way *really* worth it in the end?

Fix your eyes

> *We look not to the things that are seen but to the things that are unseen. For the things that are seen are transient, but the things that are unseen are eternal.*
>
> 2 Corinthians 4:18

You may not see it now—you may not ever see it fully in this lifetime—but what you're doing is of eternal significance. Fix your eyes there—on eternity—but be faithful here, today, . . . and tomorrow, and then next week, trusting God with the outcome as you experience the beauty and pain and struggle and wonder of walking with Him along the journey. Daily, faithfully keep walking, keep making deposits into their lives, and keep trusting that what's completely out of your control is absolutely in His. His sovereignty is our sanity, . . . and our faithfulness is enough.

Your success in God's eyes was determined the moment you said yes to this. Be free from the burden to be something for these kids that only Jesus intended *Himself* to be. Our job isn't to be their savior; it's simply to love these kids as our Savior has loved us—fully, freely, and sacrificially—and to trust Him with the rest. Give yourself some slack. No one is strutting their way through foster care; we're all limping in some way—each of us wired for struggle and worthy of grace. Certainly the kids, their families, the caseworkers, the "system," and even (sometimes especially) ourselves. At some point we come to the realization that it isn't so much "us" helping "them" as it is just "us," together—all uniquely broken humans on this journey called life, together.

I was reminded that day on our way to Chicago to enjoy the process, to soak up as much of the journey as I can. To not be so focused on where I'm trying to go that I lose sight of where I am. I needed to be reminded of that, . . . and will continue to need frequent reminders. Perhaps you will too.

The good news is that Jesus doesn't call you to control everything along the foster care journey, nor does He expect you to. He actually wants you to be okay with the fact that you can't. Your "success" as a foster parent isn't measured by your capacity to produce some certain set of outcomes; it's determined by your willingness to be faithful along the way and to trust that in the beauty, struggle, joy, and heartache of it all the journey is worth it, that Jesus is beautiful—and that so is what you're doing for these kids.

" God is more pleased by
our willingness to be
faithful along the journey of foster
care than He is concerned about
our ability to achieve a certain
outcome through it.

PERSONAL REFLECTION

1. How has your definition of "success" in foster care changed from the beginning of your journey to the present? How would you now define "success," and what steps are you taking to achieve it?

2. In what ways do you feel the need to define your success based on the outcomes you are able to produce? If you were to define your success based solely on "faithfulness," how would that change your expectations, hopes, and perceptions on your fostering journey today? To what degree, if any, would this new perspectice infuse you with a sense of relief and/or validation?

3. What would it look like for you to relinquish your expectations? What one ideal outcome might you need to let go of trying to control so that you can be more present and aware of the journey you're currently on?

GROUP DISCUSSION

1. What truth or idea stood out for you most in this session? Why?

2. In what other areas of your life have you experienced the temptation to assess your success and value based upon the outcomes *you* are able to produce? What kind of pressure has that put on you in the process? What have you learned about faithfulness and the sovereignty of God through that experience?

3. What has been the biggest surprise for you as an individual and/or couple about becoming foster parents? What did you expect to happen that hasn't, and what did you least expect that has become a significant part of the scenario?

4. What one primary expectation or perceived outcome do you need to relinquish today? How can the community around you help you in that process?

PLAN OF ACTION

1. What specific perspectives, attitudes, or ways of thinking might need to change in order for you to more effectively live out the ideas discussed in this section?

2. What specific actions or behaviors might need to change in order for you to more completely live out the ideas discussed in this section?

3. Based on what has been discussed in this section, complete the following statement as thoroughly and honestly as you can: *I will choose to honor God through this by . . .*

*I know of nothing which I would choose to have
as the subject of my ambition for life than to be
kept faithful to my God till death . . .*

CHARLES SPURGEON

CHAPTER 3

AN INVITATION INTO AN ENTIRELY NEW STORY

Foster care is just as much about pulling a child out of a broken story as it is about us being pulled into one.

Every story of abuse, neglect, and brokenness dismantles a piece of the dividing wall that once separated their normal from ours and extends the opportunity for both normals to be radically redefined forever. Their normal has been exchanged for ours, and ours for theirs. Now an entirely new normal is being written together.

In 2012 we were drawn into a story that would forever change our own. What would have been just another normal Wednesday ended up not being "normal" at all, . . . and would ultimately redefine what our normal would be from there on out.

At 7:30 that evening our first foster placement was brought to our home. We knew very little of the reality underlying her short, three-day life—just enough to feel the weight of what was taking place. She needed a safe home to stay in—and we were honored to offer ours. While love and excitement welcomed her into our home that night, we were fully aware that brokenness and tragedy had brought her there. That gravity sat upon us as we finished setting up her room, stocking up on diapers, and preparing bottles before signing paperwork at the kitchen table that would forever change the course not only of her life but of ours as well.

Reconciling two normals

In the beginning we thought foster care would simply involve taking a child from an unstable, broken place into our comfortable and safe one. We would pull a child out of her dysfunctional normal and bring her into our better one. While that is in part the case, in the end we have learned that in many ways the situation is quite the opposite. I now see that while we had welcomed this little girl into the security of our home, it was she who had actually invited us into something much deeper and more vulnerable—her story.

Although short, that story was full and extended beyond herself; we became a part of it that night, and it will remain a part of us forever. The sense of comfort and safety we had come to know as normal and natural was shattered under the weight of a brokenness and instability that came wrapped in a blanket and nestled, oblivious to all around her, in a car seat. In many ways she "wrecked" our lives that night for the better—by dismantling our conception of what we thought we knew and where we thought we were going—introducing her normal into ours and forcing us to somehow reconcile the two.

I discovered that you can't simply invite brokenness into your home and not to some degree be broken by it. You can't hold abused innocence in your arms and not on some level lose a sense of your own innocence as a result. You can't hear stories of the deep fractures in others' lives and not see the cracks in your own and understand that on some level we're all the same—broken humans in need of redemption. You can't open your heart to the vulnerable and defenseless and not be transformed by them. You can never unsee what you now see, unknow what you now know, unhear what you now hear, or unfeel what you now feel. These things will always be a part of you, and a piece of you will always be fused with them. They've become inextricably intertwined with your evolving story—an intrinsic part of your new normal.

The world as you know it is a different place—a bigger, more nuanced, more distorted place—a place somewhere between what you used to know about your little world and what you now know about the rest of it. Everything changes.

Pulling back the veil

While it can be said that foster care is the means by which we may bring about change in a child's life, it's equally true—if not more so—that foster care is a process through which God radically transforms our lives as well. Their story changes ours, not with easy and light things but with hard and heavy ones that expose the faultlines in our own stories and begin to produce new and better stories together as a result.

Our world was too small before. Our faith was too shallow, our theology too narrow, our dreams too temporary, our family too isolated, our Christianity too comfortable, our worries too finite, our relationships too homogenous and our prayers too selfish.

I'm convinced that we didn't rescue a little girl from her situation as much as a little girl rescued us from ours. She pulled back the veil around us and showed us a broken side of our world from which we had all but isolated ourselves. She pulled back the veil of our hearts as well and showed us a broken side of it we had all but ignored.

The gospel in foster care

At the heart of the gospel is a radically pursuing God who went to extravagant lengths to enter our story—a God Scripture says will flip a house upside down in order to find a lost coin (Luke 15:8–10); leave the ninety-nine sheep secure in the fold in order to chase down the wandering stray (Luke 15:3–7); throw a lavish party for a son no longer lost (Luke 15:11–32); and in the most eternally epic of proportions step out of the comfort of His glory in order to embrace us in the brokenness of our humanity—wrapping Himself in the flesh that would allow Him both to be with us and, ultimately, to be torn for us (Philippians 2:6–8). This is the heart of God decisively demonstrated through the gospel: He stepped into our brokenness to be broken by it so we wouldn't have to be broken anymore.

The beauty of foster care is showcased against the backdrop of the brokenness that surrounds it. In light of the gospel it's our privilege to crawl into the story of others, to wrap ourselves in their brokenness and willingly be broken by it—to exchange our normal for theirs and so begin to craft an entirely new and better normal together.

In the end everything changes—you change them, but perhaps more importantly, they change you.

Nothing can, will—or *should*—ever be the same again.

" While it can be said that foster care is the means by which we may bring about change in a child's life, it's equally true—if not more so—that foster care is a process through which God radically transforms our lives as well.

PERSONAL REFLECTION

1. In what ways has your normal been revolutionized and expanded through foster care? Identify specific ways in which foster care has changed you.

2. What has foster care taught you about the gospel? How has your love directed toward these kids drawn you into a deeper understanding of Christ's love for you?

3. What positive aspects are true and normal about your life now that, without foster care, wouldn't have been present? In what ways are those enhancements a gift God has given you that you might otherwise have missed the opportunity of experiencing?

GROUP DISCUSSION

1. What truth or idea stood out for you most in this session? Why?

2. In what areas of your life outside of foster care have you sought to change the life, experience, or circumstances of someone else, only to find that, in the end, your life was changed as well? In what ways was it changed?

3. In what ways has your normal been made new—enlarged and expanded—through foster care? In what specific ways has foster care changed you the most? What loss have you experienced that, while difficult in the moment, has been replaced by something exponentially better?

4. Now that you've been given a peek inside the brokenness around you, how has your view of your community and the larger world been changed? In what practical ways have you seen a passion for justice grow within you as a result of foster care?

PLAN OF ACTION

1. What specific perspectives, attitudes, or ways of thinking might need to change in order for you to more effectively live out the ideas discussed in this section?

2. What specific actions or behaviors might need to change in order for you to more completely live out the ideas discussed in this section?

3. Based on what has been discussed in this section, complete the following statement as thoroughly and honestly as you can: *I will choose to honor God through this by...*

Compassion is not a bending toward the underprivileged from a privileged position; it is not a reaching out from on high to those who are less fortunate below; it is not a gesture of sympathy or pity for those who fail to make it in the upward pull. On the contrary, compassion means going directly to those people and places where suffering is most acute and building a home there.

HENRI NOUWEN

CHAPTER 4

COUNTING THE COSTS OF FOSTERING OR ADOPTING

Every day you and I count the cost of something. We do it with clothes, food, cars, homes, extra-curricular activities, the ways in which we spend our time and energy, the number of times we hit the snooze button on the alarm clock, the friends with whom we choose to hang out, and even the ones we don't. We make these assessments intentionally but also subconsciously.

In the economy of our daily lives we are perpetually estimating the value of time, possessions, relationships, and opportunities by determining whether or not the benefit of having them in our lives will outweigh the costs required to get them, or keep them. This continuous re-evaluation of costs, worth, and ultimate value is part of our normal daily rhythm.

As I interact with people all over the country on the topics of foster care and adoption, I find these issues of cost, worth, and ultimate value to be significant—both for those who are already involved in fostering and/or adoption and those who are considering it. They're real in my own family as well, as we continually learn to embrace these tensions as a central component of who we are and what we do. We count the costs, consider the implications they will bring on our family, and ultimately—and repeatedly—have to answer a very important question: *Will it be worth it?*

Counting the costs

Nobody stands in front of family and friends on their wedding day or sits at a table signing mortgage papers without having seriously considered the implications of what they're about to do. But everyone in those situations has ultimately come to the same conclusion—it will be worth it.

The same is true for fostering and adopting—it will cost you. Maybe some money; certainly some time; definitely some energy; and absolutely some emotion, convenience, comfort, and normalcy. No one ever said "I want to foster or adopt so that my life will stay the same." Nothing will feel status quo again. Every aspect will change because of your decision. And it's important to be aware of the costs—instead of jumping in with rose-colored lenses distorting your perception of reality—and to have realistic expectations about what is to come. Because at the end of the day we accept those costs as being worth it for the gain a child will receive.

This is what Jesus has done for us: He joyfully laid down the infinite value of His own life so that we might know the immeasurable worth of being fully and unconditionally loved in Him. Foster care and adoption are beautiful expressions of that gospel. They demand a selfless, costly, and potentially painful love in order that a child can gain much as we willingly give all. As we labor to love with the same love we ourselves have received from Jesus, we do so in a cloud of uncertainties and unknowns but with the confidence of one guarantee: it's worth it. A child is worth the process and inestimably more valuable than many of the costs you are most concerned about incurring.

Outcomes vs. identity

Generally speaking, people make decisions through two primary lenses: **outcomes** and **identity**. The outcome-oriented lens filters decision-making through an assessment of costs and benefits, while the identity-oriented lens filters the process through a lens that is more intrinsically motivated by something deep within. Let me illustrate by using a classic scenario many parents present to their kids:

It's a girl's first day at her new school. She knows no one. Your daughter walks into the lunchroom with her group of friends and sees this new girl sitting alone at the end of the table. She has a decision to make—either go and engage the new girl to make her feel welcome or ignore the new girl and enjoy lunch as usual.

Her outcome-oriented paradigm of decision-making asks these questions, maybe not in these words but certainly in substance: *What will it cost me? What will it require of me? How will it make me feel? What might be the long-term effects? How can I maximize my personal satisfaction in this?* Based on the answers to these questions, she decides not to risk engaging the new girl; such a move would cost her time catching up with her friends, potentially make her feel uncomfortable conversing with someone she doesn't know, and possibly leave her feeling awkward and embarrassed.

However, her identity-oriented paradigm of decision-making asks an entirely different set of questions: *Who am I? What kind of situation is this? What does someone like me do in a situation like this? What would it cost the new girl if I didn't go and talk with her?* Based on the answers to these questions she decides to go and sit down next to the new girl. Why? Because your daughter's personal sense of identity reminds her that she is the kind of person who goes out of her way to make others feel welcome; that this is a situation in which someone is alone; and that people like herself, given the situation at hand, would go and make the new girl feel welcome.

Outcome-oriented thinking counts the costs and makes decisions that will maximize our personal satisfaction. Identity-oriented thinking still counts the costs but filters them through an entirely different set of questions, ultimately determining those costs to be worth it—to maximize not our own benefit but that of another.

As we consider the implications of engaging in foster care and adoption (either for the first time or desiring to reaffirm our decision for the fifth, sixth, or hundredth time), we do so having counted the outcome costs but not allowing our decision-making paradigm to terminate at that level. The process extends itself into an identity-oriented way of thinking: *Who am I?* I'm someone for whom Jesus laid down the infinite value of His life. *What kind of situation is this?* The kind in which these kids and families need to know the invaluable worth of being fully and unconditionally loved.

What does someone like me do in a situation like this? I count the costs and then consider them to be worth it in light of the gain someone elses stands to receive.

Our personal sense of identity, strongly formed by and rooted in the gospel, infuses us with the courage and strength to move forward even when the costs are high—because that's who we are, and that's just what people like us do.

The veil of spirituality

Let me be as honest and encouraging as I can possibly be: If you keep thinking about it, talking about it, and praying about it, that's probably a sign that you would be great at it and just need to jump in there and do it. The issue for many of us isn't whether we've been "called" to foster or adopt but what it might cost us if we actually follow through. It's easy sometimes for Christians to hide their insecurities, concerns, and fears under the veil of spiritual language, claiming that they're still "praying about it" and determining whether they've been "called" to do it, when that matter has already been resolved by God in His Word and in our hearts. At the risk of sounding unspiritual, allow me to suggest this: while the decision to follow through with involvement in foster care and/or adoption is certainly not appropriate for all, it definitely is for some, and perhaps the most spiritual thing you can do is stop praying about whether you should follow through and just do it, choosing to believe that the costs you'll incur will be worth it for the gain a child may receive.

This isn't the place everyone is at, but someone certainly is. Perhaps that someone is you.

For the better

While it's important to count the costs you may incur if you do foster or adopt, it's equally as important to consider the costs you may incur if you decide not to move forward.

Foster care and adoption have profoundly changed our family—in obvious, family-picture type ways but also in subtle, less visible, and more perspective-shifting ways. While it could be said that we have changed the lives of kids forever, I remain convinced that the impact they have had on us is exponentially greater. Of the innumerable measurement standards, following are simply two examples—our kids and our marriage—that have been forever changed through our unique foster care and adoption journey:

OUR KIDS

I used to be concerned about the effect bringing foster children into our family would have on our daughters. Would the demands detract from the attention they deserve from us? Would the inevitable bumps interrupt their routines? Would they resent us for our decision? Now, after the fact, I'm more concerned about the effect NOT bringing foster children into our home might have had on our kids. Our daughters have not been unaffected: they talk about foster care, pray often for "the fosters" before bedtime, and are excited about new kids coming into our home. As is the case with ourselves as a Mom and Dad, they can never unsee what they've seen. I'm grateful for the impact of the experience on them and hopeful that it will express itself in beautiful ways as they grow older. It has changed them for the better, and I'm convinced that our having decided not to open our home to fostering would have cost our daughters greatly.

OUR MARRIAGE

In a certain sense going through the foster care and adoption process has revealed to us a version of one another that we had yet to fully see as husband and wife. It has forced us to press Jesus more deeply into the center of our marriage and in the process has allowed us to see Him more clearly through it. We have to ask different, better questions now about our goals and priorities. We have to think about our home, our family, and our future differently because of the experience and the learning that has accompanied it. Our decision has irrevocably changed our marriage—not just in terms of what we do together but in *the way in which we are* together. We are better—not in spite of the costs but in a real sense because of them. I'm convinced that not having opened our family to foster care would have cost our marriage some of those hard but inestimably good things.

Whatever your particular situation or circumstances may be, it's quite possible that kids in foster care need your family just as much as your family needs them. It's nearly impossible to see it that way until you're in it, but it's precisely there, in the thick of the experience, that you eventually encounter the beautiful truth that foster care and adoption, more than the process by which you may change a child's life, function as a means through which God will radically transform your own. Their story changes yours forever—always and ultimately for the better. That's part of God's design in terms of how this thing is supposed to work.

We can't afford not to

When all has been said and done, let's spend less time talking about what it will cost us if we do foster or adopt and more time talking about what it will cost these kids if we don't. Kids in crisis can't afford to wait until it's most convenient for us to care for them. They simply don't have that luxury. And maybe we don't either. Perhaps the operative question we need to be asking ourselves over and over again—whether we're in the middle of the experience or still considering the possibilities for ourselves and our families—isn't "Can we afford to do this?" but rather "Can we really afford not to?" A slightly different question with significantly different implications.

At the end of the day our no will be much more difficult on them than our yes might ever be on us. So let's resolve never to neglect their perspectives in our considerations about whether or not we should proceed with fostering or adoption. What we stand to lose pales in comparison to what everyone else, especially these kids, stands to gain.

The good news for all of us is this: the gospel has the unique ability to transform costs into privileges and inconveniences into opportunities. It has the distinct capacity to completely empty us while at the same time abundantly filling us. Perhaps in the end you'll find that those costs that once concerned you have become the very catalysts that now compel you to give your all so that a child may gain much. Will it be hard? Yes. But will it be worth it? No doubt.

" Let's spend less time talking about what it will cost us if we do foster or adopt and more time talking about what it will cost these kids if we don't.

PERSONAL REFLECTION

1. What cost related to fostering seems most difficult or pressing for you right now? Why? What active steps are you taking to entrust the costs to God rather than allowing them to paralyze and prevent you from moving forward?

2. In what ways have you seen the "costs" of fostering or adopting become "benefits" for you, your family, your marriage, and your community? Be specific.

3. How has fostering or adopting drawn you into a more identity-oriented paradigm of thinking? How is that perspective influencing other areas of your life? What do you want the identity of your family to be? What are you willing to do in order to make that happen?

GROUP DISCUSSION

1. What truth or idea stood out for you most clearly in this session? Why?

2. In what other areas of your life have you seen the outcomes-oriented and identity-oriented paradigms of thinking influence your perspective, attitude, or decision-making? Explain.

3. How have you seen the "costs" of fostering or adopting become "benefits" for you, your family, your marriage and the community of people around you? Be specific.

4. By what identity and priorities do you want your family to live? What are you willing to sacrifice in order to make that a reality? Moving forward, what steps can you take to honor those family priorities on a daily basis?

PLAN OF ACTION

1. What specific perspectives, attitudes, or ways of thinking might need to change in order for you to more effectively live out the ideas discussed in this section?

2. What specific actions or behaviors might need to change in order for you to more responsibly live out the ideas discussed in this section?

3. Based on what has been discussed in this section, complete the following statement as thoroughly and honestly as you can: *I will choose to honor God through this by . . .*

The decision to grow always involves a choice between risk and comfort. This means that to be a follower of Jesus you must renounce comfort as the ultimate value of your life.

JOHN ORTBERG

CHAPTER 5

FOSTER CARE IS SPIRITUAL WARFARE

It was decision day for the baby girl we had been fostering for nearly a year—the day the court would rule on who would retain "forever" parental rights over her.

This was the culmination of months of processes, proceedings, and necessary steps taken to ensure that she would end up in the safest and most secure environment possible—ideally back home with her (now equipped and capable) mom and dad, though that wasn't looking like the probable outcome. Mom's case was swiftly ejudicated while there was still further evidence to be admitted, more testimony to be shared, and additional documents to be signed for dad's, and yet in all that we keenly felt that something far bigger was happening than merely the legal proceeding in front of us.

The tension of the unseen

What was taking place in that courtroom, just as in many other courtrooms every day all around the country, was far more than a reprimand for negligence on the part of the birth parents, the hustle of lawyers and caseworkers, or the proceedings of an overrun and under-resourced legal system. It was something infinitely bigger and deeper, spiritual and unseen. You could feel it in the room.

What was taking place that day was a battle—not between ourselves and anything or anyone else we could see but between the life of a little girl and the trajectory intended for her by an enemy who wanted to perpetuate the brokenness that had led us all there in the first place. Jesus said there is an unseen enemy seeking to steal, kill, and destroy all that God has designed to be good (John 10:10). I believe that foster care itself—the underlying need for the system—and courtrooms like the one in which we stood afford ample proof of that. Families, relationships, and bonds that God created to be healthy and nurturing have been fractured and shattered. While restoration of that good is the ultimate ideal, sometimes the brokenness perpetuates itself so that intervention of the magnitude of a hearing such as this one is required—not merely for disciplinary reasons, but for safety ones. The first goal is safety and security for a child, always.

This defenesless little one was too young to be aware that this was one of the most important days of her life—which all the more demanded someone standing where she could not and speaking what she could not on her own behalf.

I assumed that we would be silent spectators that day; the lawyers would do what they needed to do and later inform us of what we needed to do. Yet as the room fell silent I was unexpectedly called to testify before the court—there I now stood, only a few feet from this little girl's biological father, who had just endured a brutal recounting of why he was incapable of caring for a child. It was hard to sit there and listen—even if what they were saying was true. I hurt for him. I hurt for this whole day.

No longer a silent spectator, I had become an active participant. After a series of questions from the judge, his final and most significant one seemed to linger longer than the others: *Do you believe that it's in the best interest of this child for parental rights to be terminated, and, if so, is it your intention to adopt her?* That's a question I'll never forget having been asked, a question with an answer I'll always be both honored and heartbroken to have had to give: *Yes, your honor, I do, and it is our intention to adopt her if that is in her best interest.*

I knew then that none of this should have been happening—I could feel it in the room. We weren't simply engaging with a broken human story but were participating in a fractured spiritual one as well. This birth father should have been taking care of his own daughter. But now here I was, with such great privilege and joy gaining the rights over a precious little girl while a broken man stood beside me, having just lost his. While the beauty of justice had prevailed, it had done so only against the backdrop of brokenness, sadness, and loss. This wasn't how it was supposed to be. Nothing in foster care really is.

You could feel it in the air—the tension of the unseen battle was thick. Foster care is more than just a broken human story; it's a fractured spiritual one as well.

Jesus and the judge

It was in that moment that I sensed with vivid clarity a picture of what it meant for Jesus to stand before God on my behalf. To speak when I couldn't speak for myself. To stand where I couldn't stand on my own. I could imagine the heavenly scenario playing out: I'm ushered before God, the Judge, with my brokenness laid bare before Him. Jesus steps in to testify, answering the single most important question that would ultimately determine my destiny: *Jesus, do you believe that it's in the best interest of Jason for the enemy's rights to be terminated with regard to his life?* Without hesitation Jesus responds, *Yes, and I accept full responsibility for him from here on out.*

On some level this is what Scripture means when it refers to Jesus as our "advocate" (1 John 1:21) and "mediator" (1 Timothy 2:5). He stood for us when we couldn't stand on our own, spoke on our behalf when we had no words to speak. The battle has been fought for us. Jesus has won. Joy has prevailed in the midst of tragedy and heartache. We have been forever adopted into the family of God because of the work of Jesus on our behalf.

This is the gospel.

It's this gospel that calls and compels us to stand for these kids exactly where Jesus has stood for us—to physically do for them what He has spiritually done for us. It invites us to lean into the broken, not away from it, and to point to Him as the hero in all of this.

The real enemy

However, if foster care is spiritual warfare, this demands that we properly identify and position ourselves against the real and actual enemy in all of this. While these kids' situations oftentimes demand an extreme and just intervention, the enemy against whom we do battle isn't birth parents or broken systems but Satan. This is the essence of what Paul means in Ephesians 6:12 when he points out that *"we do not wrestle against flesh and blood, but against the rulers, against the authorities, against the cosmic powers over this present darkness, against the spiritual forces of evil in the heavenly places"*: spiritual warfare defined.

This is what makes it entirely possible for us to be *against* the destructive actions of biological parents but still *for* the redemptive pursuit of their souls, against what they've done but still, ultimately, for them. We are for them. They aren't the enemy—they're humans, broken people in need of redemption—just like you and me.

The true hero

One of the most liberating truths for those entrenched in the battle of foster care is this: if Satan is the real enemy, then Jesus is the ultimate hero. That means, by implication, that *we* don't have to be.

With Jesus as the hero we're freed from the burden of bearing the weight of redemption that only He was intended to carry. With Jesus as the hero foster care isn't a hopeless struggle to be endured but a vivid expression of a spiritual battle in which beauty will eventually triumph over the ugly vices of brokenness. With Jesus as the hero, the struggles we face lack the power to defeat us; they will weigh heavily upon us but have no power to break us. The enemy will seek to destroy us but can never prevail over us. This is the confidence with which we dare to intercede on behalf of these kids. This is the hope that steadies us even as the war rages on all around us.

This is spiritual warfare. This is the gospel. This is foster care.

Foster parents, thank you for doing what you're doing on behalf of these kids. In stunningly beautiful ways and with great vividness and clarity you are putting the gospel on display—standing in the gap for children, precisely in the spot where Jesus has stood for you and pointing to Him as the true hero in all of this.

As the struggle continues, know that God isn't asking you to be or do anything He alone was intended to be or do. He's simply asking you to be faithful and to trust Him with the rest, remembering every step of the way that with Jesus as the hero we don't have to be.

" Foster care is not simply
engaging in a broken
human story, but participating in
a fractured spiritual one as well.

PERSONAL REFLECTION

1. What are your thoughts on the idea that foster care entails or is necessitated by a form of spiritual warfare? Has this proven true in your experience? In what specific ways have you experienced the "battle," and what has God taught you through it?

2. Why is it important to rightly identify the enemy in foster care? Why is it important not to view birth parents, the system, caseworkers, or any other people involved in the fostering process as adversaries? Why can this at times be a difficult posture to maintain? How have you personally worked through the temptation to consider other human beings the opponents and lose sight of the real enemy in all of this? In what particular ways have you come to a deeper understanding of Ephesians 6:12 through your experiences with foster care?

3. Why is it essential to point to Jesus as the true hero in foster care? With what markers of a "savior complex" have you personally wrestled (What aspects of your attitude, perspective, or behaviors are evidence that you are operating within a "savior complex"?)? How do you combat those feelings?

GROUP DISCUSSION

1. What truth or idea stood out for you most strikingly in this session? Why?

2. As a group, read and discuss Ephesians 6:12 and discuss its implications for foster care: *"We do not wrestle against flesh and blood, but against the rulers, against the authorities, against the cosmic powers over this present darkness, against the spiritual forces of evil in the heavenly places."*

3. Has it been your experience that people will often praise you for your "heroic" work in foster care? How does that make you feel? How can you most appropriately respond to them in a way that points them to the real hero, Jesus?

4. Why is it important to rightly identify the enemy in foster care and not to view birth parents as enemies? Why can this be a difficult posture to maintain at times? What resources, practices, or behaviors help you to maintain a right posture and perspective toward the birth parents, while at the same time correctly identifying the enemy?

PLAN OF ACTION

1. What specific perspectives, attitudes, or ways of thinking might need to change in order for you to more faithfully live out the ideas discussed in this section?

2. What specific actions or behaviors might need to change in order for you to more consistently live out the ideas discussed in this section?

3. Based on what has been discussed in this section,
    complete the following statement as thoroughly
    and honestly as you can: *I will choose to honor God
    through this by . . .*

There is no neutral ground in the universe.
Every square inch, every split second is claimed
by God and counterclaimed by Satan.

C. S. LEWIS

We looked like any other couple enjoying a rare date night over chips and salsa, yet while most couples were discussing work, kids, and the latest shows on Netflix, we were weighing the cost of bringing another child into our family—a child born into extreme circumstances. A child who might have behavioral, mental, or physical issues due to neglect or abuse. A child who might reject us even as we simultaneously poured out our love. A child whom we might love fiercely . . . and yet who might ultimately leave us.

Pass the salsa, please.

When my husband, Brandon, and I began talking about foster care, our biological children were four, six, and eight years old. We thought about their needs and our family dynamics, and we considered all the ways in which foster care would cost our family. For two risk-averse people foster care seemed like the worst way to bring another child into our thriving family. Yet despite our fears, God continued to press us in that direction.

Since that initial date-night conversation we have adopted one little girl through foster care and are currently fostering her little brother and on track to adopt him as well. We always say that foster care is the best and the hardest thing we've ever done. And yes, it has cost us so much:

Time. I am a stay-at-home mom, but also an author, blogger, and speaker. Rewinding the clock to raise a baby and a toddler when our three bio kids are in grade school has greatly impacted my writing career. Brandon has also felt the stress of managing his demanding job as an attorney while pouring a significant amount of his resources and reserves into five kids. Not to mention that we're now dealing with an eleven-year age range and balancing nap times with soccer games and feeding schedules with slumber parties.

Money. Five kids. Enough said.

Emotional energy. Raising biological children causes enough emotional stress, worry, fear, anger, impatience, . . . and a whole host of other emotions. But with foster children you're not only raising kids but dealing with the baggage they bring . . . and babies are no exception. Counterintuitive as this may seem to some, we've discovered that they come to us not as blank canvases but carrying the effects of trauma that sometimes doesn't show up until years later. Add to that the CPS visits, agency visits, therapy appointments, doctors' appointments, endless paperwork, family visits, court hearings, and continuing education classes, and just the act of becoming a licensed foster parent seems daunting.

Friendships. When our daughter joined our family we were unprepared for a baby (we had originally told our agency we wanted a three- or four-year-old because we were definitely not reverting to the diaper stage . . . let alone doing it twice!). Yet when we got the call regarding a baby girl who needed to be placed within thirty minutes, we said yes! We had no diapers, clothing, or baby equipment. Nothing except arms to hold her and love to shower on her. Our community supported us so well in the form of donations: diapers, wipes, formula, clothes, bibs, blankets, pacifiers—literally overnight our house was transformed to look like Babies 'R Us.

Unfortunately, as our family has increased our community has decreased. And I get it. Whether it's the size or the noise level of our chaotic family, inviting a family of seven over to one's house for dinner can feel overwhelming. So the burden falls on us to invite people over, and sometimes this weary mom of five just doesn't have it in her to entertain guests. Consequently, relationships have waned. Connection has suffered. We're hoping this is only for a season; as we tell ourselves, "The littles won't be this little forever."

Fortunately, the benefits of foster care far outweigh the costs. Foster care has given our children a broader worldview. They are kinder, more compassionate and accepting of other kids at school. They love the chaos our big family brings to the table and talk about the kind of family they want to have some day.

The experience also creates independence in our children. With such a big family everyone pitches in. Even our two little ones do things for themselves far earlier than the older three did: clearing dishes, picking up toys, getting their own snacks, folding and putting away laundry.

Finally, Brandon and I have developed empathy—not blame—for our kids' bio mom. Yes, there have been and will continue to be consequences for her actions—consequences she suffers every day she is separated from her children. We teach our three bio kids a healthy respect and compassion for bio parents, fostering not an "us" vs. "them" mentality but a "How can we love and pray for them?" mindset.

I encourage anyone thinking about foster care to consider what the decision will cost them. But more importantly, think about the costs if you choose not to foster.

Elizabeth Oates
wife, mom of five (including three biological and two adopted through foster care), author, blogger, speaker

CHAPTER 6

REFRAMING YOUR SEASON OF STRUGGLE

Jesus' struggle on our behalf wasn't the result of His weakness but the outcome of His faithfulness. It was Him willingly choosing the cost of our great joy over the price of His immense pain.

His suffering infuses our own with meaning, and His struggle brings purpose to ours. They remind us that our work is not pointless and that the gospel is nothing if not the ability of Jesus to bring great beauty out of tragically broken things. This gospel frees us from the burden of trying to carry the weight of redemption. It reminds us that only Jesus can save and restore. Our job is simply to be faithful—expectantly, hopefully, and fervently faithful.

In your Garden of Gethsemane moments, when the weight of brokenness brings you to your knees before God and your heart cries out for a different path to redemption, you can trust that Jesus has been there before you and even now remains with you—empathizing, holding, understanding, and encouraging you to drink from the cup of sorrow and suffering again and again. The road to redemption is paved with the stones of suffering, and only the strongest allow themselves to be weakened by the weight of the cross they must carry along the way. Count yourself, as He does, among the strongest—not in spite of the weakness you now feel but because of and through it.

Jesus is worth it

Thank you for your faithfulness even in the midst of this season you're going through. Thank you for choosing to count the joy of these kids as worth the cost of your pain. No one sees your struggle as weakness. No one dares question your resolve. They see it as brave and inspiring, and no doubt God views it as beautiful—because He sees Jesus all over it, in it, and through it.

God is using you, a mere human, to help solve a seemingly insurmountable human problem. Confusion, frustration, and exhaustion are inevitable and unavoidable, but He is faithful and good and right there with you. The gospel doesn't guarantee that everything will be easy, but it does infuse us with the hope that no matter what, Jesus is worth it—and so is what you're doing for these kids.

Reframing the struggle

Your brokenness isn't a sign of failure, but an outcome of faithfulness. Jesus knows exactly how that feels. Your struggle isn't a sign of weakness, but an expression of faithfulness. It shows that you care, even when it's hard. And your exhaustion isn't a sign of defeat, but of an overflow of faithfulness. It means that you're giving all so that a child might gain much—and that's remarkable. There's always another side to our struggle—a hopeful, encouraging one, if we're only willing to reframe it and see it that way.

Through what appears to be your weakness Christ is making His strength abundantly known. Paul understood this, declaring in 2 Corinthians 12:9–10, *"I will boast all the more gladly in my weaknesses, so that the power of Christ may rest upon me. . . . For when I am weak, then I am strong."*

The apostle flips the script on how we're to understand our weaknesses. The world urges us to conceal or camouflage them, to avoid them and not to acknowledge or talk about them. The world considers them shameful, yet Paul boasts about them. Why? Because far from being a source of shame they've become for him a platform upon which to showcase the power of God. Weakness isn't for us as Christians a road to avoid but the very pathway through which God has chosen to bring great beauty out of tragic brokenness.

It's not something that disqualifies us from being used by Him. In fact, it might be one of the very things which qualifies us the most. Consider, if God's power is put on display most in our weakness, then perhaps those times when we feel like "we can't" are actually some of His greatest gifts of grace to us.

Sometimes it isn't one big crisis but a series of trivial issues collected over time that eventually starts to feel too heavy to bear—frustrations like not being able to be present at three appointments at one time, an unexpected meltdown by a child in the grocery store that turned what should have been a quick trip into something much more impactful, a no-show from the caseworker, or frustrations with the certification, paperwork and on-going inspections process. It's the daily, consistent, habitual inconveniences and interruptions that eventually cause us to step back and ask whether there might not be some other, less irritating, path to redemption. Can we keep going at this pace? Is it really making a difference, and will it ultimately be worthwhile?

Sometimes, of course, the issue is far more serious— one of those "I feel like my soul is dying" kind of struggles. Exhaustion has made its home into the innermost recesses of who we are, and there seems to be no way for it to find its way back out. While this, we admit in our weaker moments, is what we signed up for, in so many ways that isn't the case. We didn't ask for the life to be sucked out of us like this.

In the midst of your weakness and the wake of your struggle, "success" as a foster or adoptive parent isn't measured by your capacity to keep everything in order but by your ability to trust that even in the chaos Jesus is beautiful—and that even in the mess, so is what you're doing for these kids.

Okay to not be okay

Kids from hard places don't need perfect, polished parents but parents who are strong enough to be weak and who are honest and real. Maybe today you don't need to pretend that you've got it all together. Maybe today is your day to finally be okay with the fact that it's okay to not be okay. If there's room in the gospel for these kids' redemption, there must also be room for yours. Perhaps you simply need to give yourself that space today. Maybe the best thing you can do for your kids right now is to spend some time pressing into Jesus for your own sake, right here and right now. It's okay to not be okay; it just isn't okay to stay there forever. That's where the gospel thrives, where true strength is found, and where Jesus patiently waits to remind us that, in the end, it isn't about us but about Him.

It's okay to not be okay; it's just not okay to stay that way. Sometimes the most spiritual thing you can do is read a good book, hire a babysitter, go to counseling, spend a care-free evening out with friends or just take a nap. No one wins if you lose yourself. Everyone wins if you're healthy, whole and regularly taking steps to attend to those deep, inner life things that bring you fulfillment, healing and refreshment. Self-care is not selfish; it's spiritual. It's one of the bravest, most difficult yet profoundly important things you can do along your foster care and adoption journey.

Thank you for doing what you're doing. You may not be okay right now, but you are brave—and that in itself is okay. You may not be okay right now, but you are inspiring, and that's more than okay. You may not be okay right now, but what you're doing is nonetheless beautiful, not because you always have to be but because Jesus always is, and if that's all you have to cling to right now—that's certainly okay too.

Perhaps, in the end, the thing that will surprise you most about your foster care journey will be YOU! Hidden weaknesses will be exposed but inner strengths will be revealed in ways you otherwise would have never discovered. This is grace.

" Your brokenness isn't a
sign of failure, but an
outcome of faithfulness. Jesus
knows exactly how that feels.

PERSONAL REFLECTION

1. In what ways has the foster care journey forced you to embrace your weakness as a platform upon which the power of God can be put on display?

2. If foster care magnifies and maximizes the divine strength underlying our weaknesses, in what ways have you been surprised by your resulting strength and resolve? In what areas have you seen your weaknesses most exposed? Can you specifically identify your greatest strengths? Your most problematic weaknesses?

3. Rather than viewing our deficits as sources of insecurity, Scripture elevates our weaknesses as platforms upon which the strength of Christ can be showcased. In what ways have you seen and experienced His strength operating through and around you during the course of your foster care journey?

GROUP DISCUSSION

1. What truth or idea stood out for you most strongly in this session? Why?

2. In what specific area(s) of foster parenting have you found yourself to be "weakest" and God "strongest"?

3. What does the enemy want you to believe about your weaknesses? How is that different from what God says about them? Cite an example of your weakness being an asset, as opposed to a liability, in terms of your ability to effectively foster parent.

4. What role does community play for you as you navigate through your strengths and weaknesses in the area of fostering? How can you be more transparent with your struggles moving forward—not to wallow in them but to leverage them as platforms upon which the power of God can be put on display?

PLAN OF ACTION

1. What specific perspectives, attitudes, or ways of thinking might need to change in order for you to better live out the ideas discussed in this section?
2. What specific actions or behaviors might need to change in order for you to more effectively live out the ideas discussed in this section?
3. Based on what has been discussed in this section, complete the following statement as thoroughly and honestly as you can: *I will choose to honor God through this by . . .*

NOTE: *As we discuss weaknesses, struggles, and the freedom to not be okay, it's imperative that we highlight the importance of seeking professional counseling when it's needed. Your mental health as a foster parent is paramount, not just in terms of your capacity to serve the kids in your care but first and foremost to be a healthy man/woman, husband/wife, mom/dad, and Christ-follower. In Him our weaknesses are no longer sources of shame, and seeking the professional help you need isn't either.*

The deepest need you and I have in weakness and adversity is not quick relief, but the well-grounded confidence that what is happening to us is part of the greater purpose of God.

JOHN PIPER

CHAPTER 7

REDEFINING SUCCESS AND FAILURE AS A FOSTER PARENT

You don't have to be perfect parents in order to be perfect foster parents. Let's read that sentence again: You don't have to be perfect parents in order to be perfect foster parents. Inherent in the role is the pressure to be amazing because "you are doing something amazing" (what others may have said of you); that's an expectation no human can live up to, nor should you ever have to try.

Foster parents are neither saints nor heroes nor spiritual rock stars. We're humans, real moms and dads who struggle, stumble, and mess up. We get annoyed, frustrated, and depleted. We don't have all the answers and don't even know the right questions to ask much of the time.

Give yourself some grace

Cut yourself some slack. It isn't, after all, your job to be the savior of these kids but simply to love them as your Savior has loved you: fully, sacrificially, painstakingly, and honestly.

God didn't call you to this because He thought you could handle it, and He certainly isn't surprised by the fact that there are those times when you can't. He called you to this to show what *He* can do through you—not just handle it but accomplish beautiful things through it—through you. He is using you, a mere human, to help resolve a seemingly insurmountable human problem. Confusion, frustration, and exhaustion are inevitable and unavoidable, but He is faithful and good and right there with you, even on those days when you aren't certain you can handle it any longer.

Redefining failure

God doesn't expect us to fix the kids who've come to us from hard places, to save them or help them pretend that nothing tragic has ever happened in their lives. He simply asks us to show up and love them. That love will be costly and difficult at times. It will stretch you at times almost to the breaking point, but it will also fill, strengthen, and drive you. Our calling is to love *like* Him because we have first been loved *by* Him—and to trust Him with the outcomes.

Failure in foster care is defined not by our inability to love a child perfectly but by our failure to show up and love a child at all.

By the very nature of your decision to love, you *are not* failing. You're succeeding, no matter how difficult this may be at times. Free yourself from the burden to be everything the child needs. Instead, find peace in your obedience to the call to be faithful in what you do.

Redefining success

Let me reiterate, the good news is that Jesus doesn't call you to control everything in the foster care process, nor does He expect you to. He actually wants you to be okay with the fact that you can't. Your "success" as a foster parent is not measured by your capacity to keep everything in order but by your ability to trust that even in the chaos Jesus is true and constant and near and beautiful—and that even in the mess your efforts are by no means failing, but your love is indeed succeeding beyond what you could possibly fathom.

Beauty in the brokenness

Every aspect of foster care is composed of equal parts good and bad, joy and sorrow, beauty and brokenness. It's a good day when a child is placed in your home, a transition representing safety, security, and an opportunity for that child to be loved and cared for in a way they likely wouldn't have experienced otherwise. It's indeed a good day when a child is placed in your home—but it's at the same time a really bad day: a day marred by hurt and brokenness, a day in which, though so much gain has been made available to a child, loss has ultimately led them to this point. In too many cases a recurring cycle of family brokenness has perpetuated itself into the lives of the next generation—abuse, neglect, and/or abandonment have become a part of their story. They didn't ask for this. This was all unjustly handed to them by those who were most responsible to protect them.

While the opportunity to love these kids is excellent and wonderful, the circumstances that bring them to us are far from excellent and wonderful. The call to foster parenting exposes us to brokenness and demands from us a humble and gracious perspective in order for us to rightly and lovingly care for these vulnerable kids.

Their tragedy over our eagerness

As excited as we may be about fostering kids, we can be fairly certain that they're less than excited about becoming foster kids. It isn't our personal sense of excitement, but their personal tragedy—their heartache—that drives our efforts. It's about our desire to see good come out of bad. Our willingness to embrace what is broken and do whatever it takes to bring healing. That's why we do what we do. It has to be.

Celebrate the opportunity to open your home to kids in need, knowing that if this ends up being for just a few days or an entire lifetime you've been given the unique opportunity to offer them something special: love. At the same time, never let your excitement about being involved in foster care override your sensitivity to the tragic realities that cause the system to exist in the first place.

There will be days that are anything but exciting— that are, in fact, very, very hard. But we don't go into this expecting it to be easy; ironically, we do it *because it's hard.* It hurts to see kids unwittingly, and unwillingly, thrust into such a position. It hurts to see families broken. It's hard to love kids who have been deeply wounded by circumstances and situations outside their control—or yours. It's hard to love kids who will likely leave—hard to figure out how to hold them tightly and loosely at the same time.

We do this because it's hard—the kind of hard that will force you on several occasions to step back and ask yourself an important and necessary question: "Why are we doing this?" You may be experiencing one of those days—or seasons—right now. It's in moments like this that you must press more deeply into Jesus and your belief that the gospel is nothing if not a demonstration of His ability to bring great beauty out of tragic brokenness. What appeared to be His greatest defeat on the cross was in fact His ultimate victory, that shining moment when beauty triumphed—not in the absence of brokenness but in its devastating wake.

That's why you're doing this. This is why we do foster care. Because of the Cross. It has to be.

At the end of our days

This is foster care—intervening into dark places in order to bring light into them. It's about advocating the cause of the helpless, seeking justice for the defenseless, and maintaining the rights of the oppressed. This is what Jesus has done for us. We, therefore, are compelled to do the same for them.

At the end of our days we'll measure the success of our years not by the places we went or the things we created but in terms of the people we've loved and the lives we've impacted for good. Foster care affords you the opportunity to successfully spend your life to that end.

Thank you for doing what you do. God is using you to love in some of the hardest places and through some of the most difficult situations. The success of your love won't be determined by your capacity to fix things but by your willingness to give. The expectation isn't that your love will always pull people out of a broken place but that it will at least be willing to walk with them in and through it—just like Jesus walks with us in ours.

Press on. Be successful. It's worth it.

> **The expectation isn't that your love will always pull people out of a broken place but that it will at least be willing to walk with them in and through it.**

PERSONAL REFLECTION

1. In what areas of life outside foster care has God called you to something you couldn't handle on your own? What did you learn about failure and success through that experience? What was the outcome? What did you learn through it about God and yourself?

2. In what ways have you seen your excitement about fostering tempered by the reality of brokenness that surrounds the whole process? How has that "tempering" process been helpful for you? How is your call to foster parenting affirmed and reaffirmed even on those days that are anything but exciting? How have you seen the faithfulness of God toward you in this journey on those days when you've found it necessary to step back and ask "Why are we doing this?"

3. In what ways has foster care forced you to let go of your own ideal picture of success? How has it forced you to redefine failure? Helped shape a vision for how you will "successfully spend your life" in the future?

GROUP DISCUSSION

1. What truth or idea stood out for you most memorably in this session? Why?

2. In what other areas of life have you experienced the reality that there's never "a perfect time" to obey— that you might never be fully ready to step into some

worthwhile endeavor? To what specific task was God calling you even though it wasn't the easiest, most convenient, or most comfortable for you? What was the outcome?

3.   Describe a time when you got to the point in your fostering journey at which you were asking "Why are we doing this?" What brought you there? What did you learn through the experience—about yourself, about God, and about His call to this venture? Looking back, why is being brought to that point "important and necessary" at times?

4.   What do you struggle most to keep in order throughout the fostering process? Perhaps it's your time, your emotions, or your perspective. How has God helped you redefine success and failure through those places of chaos? In what ways have you seen Jesus as beautiful and been reminded of the beauty in what *you* are doing for these kids?

PLAN OF ACTION

1.   What specific perspectives, attitudes, or ways of thinking might need to change in order for you to more effectively live out the ideas discussed in this section?

2.   What specific actions or behaviors might need to change in order for you to more successfully live out the ideas discussed in this section?

3.   Based on what has been discussed in this section, complete the following statement as thoroughly and honestly as you can: *I will choose to honor God through this by . . .*

Our greatest fear should not be of failure,
but of succeeding at things in life that don't really matter.

FRANCIS CHAN

CHAPTER 8

LOVING OUT OF OUR POVERTY

When speaking of the widow's meager offering in comparison to that of the rich (Luke 21:1–4), Jesus said, *"Truly, I tell you, this poor widow has put in more than all of them. For they all contributed out of their abundance, but she out of her poverty put in all she had."*

What a provocative statement! And what encouragement each of us can take from Jesus' assessment that the value of the widow's offering was measured not in terms of quantity but of quality and humility; not by size but by the degree of sacrifice. Notice that Jesus doesn't discredit the offerings of the wealthy but simply redefines that of the poor. In that moment He stops and essentially says to all within earshot, "Hey, there's something truly profound going on here that I don't want you to miss."

She gave far less than any one of the others but gave all she had, and He calls it "more."

Amazing.

A deficiency in our souls

If the fostering and adoption journey has taught me one thing, it's this: that we love these kids out of our poverty, not our abundance. We know going in that we can offer a certain set of resources that might make their lives more comfortable, and hopefully more enjoyable. But we quickly learn that this isn't ultimately what it's all about.

Somehow their stories, and the gravity of our becoming a part of them, expose a deficiency not in our stuff but in our souls. It isn't so much that *we* are bringing these kids out of their "poverty" into our "abundance" but that *they* are in many ways rescuing us from our "abundance" by exposing us to our own "poverty." That, then, becomes the place from which we love them—a deficient, broken, impoverished place within us that I'm convinced Jesus looks at and says, "Yes! That's it right there! That's the 'more' I'm looking for."

Loving out of our poverty

Loving out of our poverty feels small and insignificant at times—as though all we have to offer to the kids and families we are loving is two small coins. We feel as though we're failing and convince ourselves that we can't handle it. We feel as though we aren't doing enough, as though we don't have what it takes. Yet somehow Jesus flips the script on that small offering and declares it "more"—more valuable, more significant, more meaningful, more impactful, and more beautiful than we could possibly measure. In the gospel our poverty is no longer a source of shame but rather the platform upon which the sufficiency and abundance of God can be made most visible—not only in the lives of the kids we're loving but in our own lives as well. It's that beautiful and yet hard and vulnerable place that postures us the lowest, . . . and ultimately points to Him as the greatest.

God isn't surprised by our weakness or taken aback by our inability. He isn't embarrassed by what little we have to offer and is certainly not disappointed when He counts it up in the offering box. He's absolutely, unequivocally, and unconditionally proud of our gift—all two small coins of it at times—because He knows it's a measure of something much deeper and less tangible, a measure not just of all that we have in our hands but of all that we are in our hearts. And it's at that place, right there, that Jesus stops and says, "Hey, there's something truly profound going on here that I don't want you to miss."

Have you ever felt like all you had to give into this journey was the equivalent of two small coins? Jesus looks at it and calls it "more."

What you're doing is infinitely more in God's eyes than what it feels or looks like today or how well or how poorly you think you're doing. What you are doing is more than the sum total of all those good things the enemy wants to convince you you're failing to accomplish today. What you are doing is so much more than whatever it is you're telling yourself you aren't doing today.

I have no doubt that Jesus looks on you today, no matter the celebrations or struggles that have punctuated your journey, and pronounces, "Yes . . . that's it right there!"

What you are doing is more!

> **In the gospel our poverty is no longer a source of shame but rather the platform upon which the sufficiency and abundance of God can be made most visible.**

PERSONAL REFLECTION

1. In what other areas of life, beyond foster care, have you seen God's radical redefining of "more" proven true?

2. In what ways have you encountered and confronted your own "poverty" in your fostering journey?

3. What hope do you have in the gospel, and in God's radical redefining of what constitutes "more" in His kingdom? How is His definition of "more" different from the world's understanding of "more"? To what unique aspects of the gospel must you cling in order to maintain a proper perspective on your weakness, your "poverty," and Jesus' definition of "more"?

GROUP DISCUSSION

1. What truth or idea stood out for you most in this session? Why?

2. As a group, read together Luke 21:1–4: *"Jesus looked up and saw the rich putting their gifts into the offering box, and he saw a poor widow put in two small copper coins. And he said, 'Truly, I tell you, this poor widow has put in more than all of them. For they all contributed out of their abundance, but she out of her poverty put in all she had to live on.'"*

    What stands out for you most strikingly in this story? In what other areas of life, beyond foster care, have you seen God's radical redefining of "more" proven true? Why is this new perspective especially relevant and encouraging in your fostering journey?

3.   In what specific area of foster parenting have you found yourself to be most "impoverished"? How have you seen the power and faithfulness of God showcased through your deficiency?

4.   If your friends, concerned that they might not have "enough" of what it takes to become foster parents, were to ask you for counsel, what would you say to them? How would Jesus' redefining of "more" offer them hope, encouragement, and motivation?

PLAN OF ACTION

1.   What specific perspectives, attitudes, or ways of thinking might need to change in order for you to more effectively live out the ideas discussed in this section?

2.   What specific actions or behaviors might need to change in order for you to more meaningfully live out the ideas discussed in this section?

3.   Based on what has been discussed in this section, complete the following statement as thoroughly and honestly as you can: *I will choose to honor God through this by . . .*

It isn't your weakness that will get in the way of God's working through you, but your delusions of strength. His strength is made perfect in our weakness! Point to His strength by being willing to admit your weakness.

PAUL DAVID TRIPP

CHAPTER 9

BUSYNESS, OBEDIENCE, AND THE PERFECT TIME TO FOSTER OR ADOPT

I've found something to be true of myself at times, and the more I talk with others the more I find it to be equally true of them. It's the idea that my busyness is something to boast about, as though it were a badge of honor to be worn so that others can see how important, productive, and crucial I am to the world around me.

"How have things been going?" I'm often asked.

"Man, it's been busy lately," I often reply.

This is true of all of us at times. While touting our busyness and toting it around like a trophy, could it be that we're using it as a scapegoat? "It isn't *me*," we clarify. "It's my busyness that's preventing me from really engaging my neighbors, pursuing my dreams, plugging in to my church, or really giving myself to worthwhile things I'm passionate about"—translation, those things we would most certainly do if life weren't so crazy busy all the time, right?

The right kind of busy

Don't get me wrong, there are seasons of life that are nothing short of chaotic and hectic. We've got a lot on our plates, and most of it is important—long-term responsibilities we can't neglect and urgent tasks that just have to get done. All of us frequently find ourselves in such real and legitimate places. The truth is that our busyness, far from being a trophy, is often times a ball-and-chain.

But there are also times when, if we're honest, our problem isn't that we're busy per se but that we're busy with things that don't really matter—or with too many things that do matter.

Sometimes it isn't the pressing responsibilities in front of us that detract from our ability to engage with such opportunities. It's actually the opposite. It's choosing lesser things, like three hours of our favorite Netflix show every day, that limits our capacity to engage with these and other excellent opportunities before us. I don't believe that being busy is in and of itself a problem—but I do believe that being busy with the wrong things is. I don't know about you, but I want to lay down my head every night exhausted, not because I've expended my energy that day on things that don't matter but because I've spent myself on other valid things that do. The first is exhausting and unfulfilling. The second is just as exhausting, but far more satisfying.

At still other times our problem isn't that we're busy doing the wrong things but that we're simply overextending ourselves, feeling ourselves incapable of saying no to too many right things. You may well be able to assess the landscape of your current time management and determine that there really isn't much waste—that you're spending the majority of your time each day and the majority of your days each week on "good" things—like volunteering at church, meeting with the local book club, sitting on the PTA board, or helping oversee the construction of a new playground in your neighborhood park. While there's nothing inherently wrong with any of the individual things you're doing, you at some point begin to feel as though you've spread yourself too thin—accomplishing many things decently but not really delving deeply into any one thing with the commitment you'd like to offer it. Although this is equally as insidious a trap as spending your time on things that don't really matter, it's harder to identify and acknowledge because you aren't necessarily doing anything wrong; you're just doing too much of what's "right." Perhaps the best recourse would be to determine which good things it's time to decline or step down from in order to free up the economy of your time for investing in other, more substantial and currently meaningful good things.

When my wife and I began the foster care training process, we, like you, were busy: three young kids, a new church plant, commitments here, and obligations there. And I must confess that I used our busyness as a crutch for disobedience. I knew that God was inviting us to venture out onto the fostering journey, but I also knew how legitimately busy we were. It just wasn't "the right time, God." Or so I thought . . .

Choosing yes

It's quite possible that the perfect season of life you're waiting for will never come. When will the frenetic pace of life *really* slow down enough for you to willingly choose to make it crazy and busy all over again by fostering or adopting?

Ask yourself this: What circumstances in your life would need to be in place in order for you to determine that it is in fact the right time to foster or adopt?

Have you considered the possibility that the parameters you've set to determine your readiness may be too narrow? What if they leave no space for you to actually ever feel ready? What if you're more ready now than you realize?

This isn't to disregard the very real and legitimate issues you need to consider before fostering or adopting: like the health of your marriage, the needs of your kids, your finances, and your emotional capacity to bear the weight of broken stories and love the children who come from them. These issues must be taken into account when you're considering whether to foster or adopt. However, I find that for most people it all boils down to issues of time, busyness, and margins. "We want to foster or adopt," many say, "but life is just so busy right now." Again, this concern may well be valid, but too often it can be a smokescreen.

I'm not in a position to offer counsel with regard to what's right for you at any given time—only you, through an honest examination of your own heart and evaluation of your circumstances, can determine that. I am suggesting that you take the time to ask yourself the hard and pressing questions and consider that in the grand scheme of things there's never going to be a "perfect" time to foster or adopt, just a lot of opportunities to say yes despite the many reasons you may be able to offer to say no. I suppose that faith, on some level, can be defined in similar terms—as choosing to say yes despite all the valid-sounding reasons you have for saying no.

Let me encourage and then challenge you

First, the encouragement. Your life is probably crazy busy. In all likelihood, if you're considering this kind of endeavor and reading this book in the first place, you're just that kind of individual/couple. But you're capable of handling far more than you could possibly imagine—even if it doesn't feel that way right now. The good news is that Jesus neither calls nor expects you to control everything in the foster care or adoption process; He actually wants you to be okay with the fact that you can't. As I've stated before (and it bears repeating), your success won't be measured by your capacity to keep everything in order but hinges on your ability to trust that even in the chaos Jesus is beautiful—and so is what you have to offer these kids. He doesn't expect you to understand it all now; He's simply asking you to trust Him with the next step, and then the next, and the next . . .

Now for the challenge. Kids in crisis can't afford to wait until it's most convenient for you to care for them. *Their* need is for *you* to stop rationalizing about what you sense God is calling you to do—and just do it. Again, as I've stated before, your no is a lot harder on them than your yes will ever be on you. Perhaps these kids need your family as much as your family needs them. One is afforded comfort and security, quite possibly for the first time in their life, while the other is freed from comfort and security and as a result actually finds life. In Jesus' words, *"Whoever would save his life will lose it, but whoever loses his life for my sake will find it"* (Matthew 16:25). In what is perhaps one of the most counterintuitive and countercultural statements our Lord ever made, He tells us that we discover what life is truly about when we willingly lose ourselves and relinquish our prerogatives on it, as He did, for the the sake of someone else's gain. Hard? Undoubtedly. Worth it? Absolutely. What you stand to lose pales in comparison to what everyone, including yourself, stands to gain through the arrangement. To reiterate, there's never an ideal time to foster or adopt—just a lot of opportunities to say yes to losing yourself despite the many good reasons you have to say no.

Jesus is better

Before someone pulls a Jesus-juke and insists that there *is* in fact a perfect time to foster or adopt—as in, when God says to—permit me to be very clear: I agree, but be aware that He may also make it clear to you when it *isn't* the easiest, most convenient, or most comfortable time for you. One way or the other, obedience when you sense that the time is right (and when He doesn't tell you it isn't) is about considering the costs and choosing to believe that Jesus is better—that what He wants you to do for these kids is worth the cost and that He'll take care of you every step of the way.

If you're someone who keeps wondering about fostering or adopting, talking about it, and praying about it, you're probably someone who just needs to do it . . . and most likely somebody who'll be great at it. I understand that I may not be writing to your particular circumstances right now. No book, blog, or article can ever address the uniquenesses of *everyone's* situation. It is, however, written to those who currently are or have ever been guilty of rationalizing, justifying, and delaying obedience for the sake of their personal comfort and convenience.

Really, it's written to myself, the chief of all rationalizers and delayers.

But maybe also to you. Only you know.

> **There's never going to be a "perfect" time to foster or adopt, just a lot of opportunities to say yes despite the many reasons you may be able to offer to say no.**

PERSONAL REFLECTION

1. In what other areas of life have you experienced the reality that there's never a perfect time to obey and that you might never be fully ready to step into some worthwhile endeavor? To what specific task or activity has God called you even though it wasn't the easiest, most convenient, or most comfortable track for you? What was the outcome?

2. What compelled you to say yes to foster care despite all the reasons you may have had for saying no? What continues to compel you to confirm your yes? If you haven't yet voiced your yes, what apprehensions might be holding you back? What circumstances would need to be in place in your life in order for you to deem it the right time to foster or adopt?

3. In what ways have the demands of foster care forced you to let go of lesser priorities? What, specifically, have you had to lose in order to embark on this journey? In what ways has going through that process shown you that Jesus is better?

GROUP DISCUSSION

1. What truth or idea stood out for you most clearly in this session? Why?

2. In what areas of life besides foster care have you experienced the reality that there's "never a perfect time" to obey and that you might never be fully "ready" to step into something? What specific thing was God calling you to even though it wasn't the easiest, most convenient or comfortable for you? What was the outcome?

3. How has the process of foster care forced you to let go of lesser priorities in your life? What specific activities and interests have you had to relinquish in order to fully participate in the fostering and/or adoption process? How have you personally experienced that Jesus as better than those things and that caring for these kids is worth the cost of letting other activities go?

4. Recall what compelled you to say yes to foster care in the beginning. Why is it that you continue along this journey? If your best friends were considering foster care, how would you counsel them through their rationalizations and concerns related to the relinquishing of lesser priorities and the opportunity to say yes despite all of the legitimate reasons for saying no? How does your hypothetical counsel toward them encourage and inspire you today?

PLAN OF ACTION

1. What specific perspectives, attitudes, or ways of thinking might need to change in order for you to more effectively live out the ideas discussed in this section?

2. What specific actions or behaviors might need to change in order for you to better live out the ideas discussed in this section?

3. Based on what has been discussed in this section, complete the following statement as thoroughly and honestly as you can: *I will choose to honor God through this by...*

*The best measure of a spiritual life
is not its ecstasies but its obedience.*
OSWALD CHAMBERS

CHAPTER 10

THE BEST THING YOU CAN DO FOR YOUR MARRIAGE

NOTE: If you're married, it is highly recommended that you read this section and walk through the following "personal reflection" and "plan of action" questions together with your spouse.

One of the busiest seasons of our marriage coincided with the beginning of our foster care journey. With three young kids already, a full schedule, and high demands at work, the responsibilities and obligations that came with bringing another child into our home were overwhelming at times. Not just any child, but a child with uniquely special needs, along with a schedule entailing court hearings, parent visits, home studies, and mounds of paperwork. We found it all too easy to become so consumed by the juggling act of getting things done as husband and wife to the neglect of some of the most important questions—not "*What do we need to do?*" but "*How are we doing? Are we 'good'? Are we connected? Are we as together as we need to be?*"

The enemy certainly didn't want the two of us to be a united front. And he doesn't want you to be either.

The truth is, we don't just bring foster children into our homes; we also bring them into our marriages. And the weight of caring for kids from hard places can either break our marriages or strengthen them. In the end we want to be better connected and to experience greater depths of intimacy as a result. But these outcomes don't just "happen"; they must be intentionally pursued, cultivated, and fought for.

The enemy's bullseye

Satan has a destructive plan for your marriage, yet his tactics are often subtle and unseen. The Bible tells us that he maneuvers like a "roaring lion" (1 Peter 5:8) and disguises himself as "an angel of light" (2 Corinthians 11:14). Sneaky, hidden, deceiving. Your obedience to God doesn't insulate you from his attacks; in fact, it exposes you all the more.

The opportunity to engage in foster care is in part a call to purposefully, willingly, sacrificially, and joyously position yourself and your marriage in the crosshairs of the enemy's attack. As you stand, together as husband and wife, in the gap for these kids, you'll find yourselves beaten, battered, and bruised along the way. And yet, in a beautifully upside down kind of way, that's exactly why you're doing what you're doing: willingly taking the blows so these kids will no longer have to.

You are living, breathing, crying, and walking out the gospel in the lives of vulnerable kids on a daily basis, all the while exposing yourself and your marriage to spiritual warfare unlike any you've ever experienced. Satan believes that if he can crack your marriage under the weight of foster care he can probably cause the whole structure around you to crumble. That's his aim.

Jesus at the center

That's why the best thing you can do for your marriage while engaged in foster care is to resist making it all about foster care. In the midst of paperwork, training hours, court hearings, doctor appointments, parent visits, caseworker meetings, and the unpredictability of parenting children from hard and traumatic places, it's easy to allow the activity of foster care to replace the intimacy of marriage. This is why Jesus *in your marriage* has to take precedence even over Jesus *in your mission.* The center of our connection with one another within our marriage, after all, isn't *what we do* together in foster care but *who we are* together in Jesus, which then overflows into what we do—from the inside out. Everyone wins when we operate out of this identity: our marriage wins when we love Jesus first, our kids win when they have a mom and dad centered on Him, and any child we bring into that environment wins for obvious reasons. If your marriage is "off" your mission can only go so far. It isn't selfish to put it first sometimes. It's smart.

Now more than ever before you are a team, fighting in tandem for justice, loving the helpless as one, speaking in stereo for the defenseless, and banding together against the one who wants to destroy it all. The inevitable demands and setbacks will take you to hard places together, expose broken places within each of you, and produce intimacy and connection between you that you might otherwise never have the opportunity to experience. Satan wants the mission of foster care to break your marriage, but God has the capacity to build your marriage through it, if you'll allow Him to.

How do you go about this? Let me suggest a few practical steps you can take that will go a long way toward cultivating the space and time necessary for your marriage to stay rooted in Jesus and each other:

PRAY TOGETHER

It's impossible either to fully explain or to overestimate the importance of this practice. You are fighting a spiritual battle together against powers and principalities that can be effectively combatted only through prayer. Consistent time in prayer, both together and separately, along with time in the Word of God, is by far the most crucial thing you can do to ward off the enemy and keep Jesus central.

DATE EACH OTHER

I know, I know, I know . . . it can sometimes be impossible to find certified babysitters. Let me suggest a few possibilities. If such providers are available to you, use them. If not, ask friends and family to take on that role. Get creative. Date at home when the kids are asleep, at school, or with friends. Maximize the time you have, whenever it is you have it.

DON'T ALWAYS TALK ABOUT FOSTER CARE

We've all seen the couple portrayed on the television sitcom that goes on a date, tries not to talk about their kids, . . . and fails miserably. Don't be that couple. It's hard—but important—in this setting to connect on other topics. Be intentionally relational (*How are you doing?*) not just functional (*What do we need to do?*).

LIVE IN COMMUNITY

It's incredibly easy to begin to feel isolated in foster care. Most people around you don't understand the unique nuances of the endeavor in which you're involved. Find people who do. It's essential for you to be connected to others who can help point you and your marriage back to Jesus. People you can laugh and cry with, and with whom you can take a mental break from foster care. Your marriage can't handle this alone.

GIVE EACH OTHER BREAKS

The health of a marriage is determined by the health of each individual in the marriage. Husbands, make space for your wife to be alone, be refreshed, go out with friends, pamper herself, etc. Take the kids on an outing upon occasion and free up her schedule. Wives, do the same for your husbands. Support each other's personal health; this will only make you better together.

A new version of our marriage

Over time I began to see a part of my wife I had never glimpsed before, just as she was coming to witness a new side to her husband. I saw a beauty in the love with which she cared for a baby girl who wasn't her own. I saw a woman who felt a deep empathy toward this child's birth mom that only she as a mother could have experienced. She saw a shift in me as well—a softening in terms of my capacity to fall in love with a child who would likely leave us at some point. The experience opened my heart and emotions in new, profound, and surprising ways.

The hard side of foster care has been real and raw. We've grieved together over letting go of kids we deeply love. We've struggled together over how best to care for the birth mom of our now adopted daughter. We've looked at each other in complete confusion as a teenage girl locked herself in the bathroom and then proceeded to cut off all her hair because she just couldn't come up with a more productive way to cope with her feelings. We've wrestled together through the tension between our pull toward comfort and complacency and our conviction that kids need homes and that ours should be one of them. The real and raw of foster care have revealed to us a version of each other that we had yet to fully encounter in our marriage. It has forced us to press Jesus more deeply into the center of our marriage—in ways we might never otherwise have experienced—and as a result has allowed us to see Him more clearly through it. It has undoubtedly changed our marriage, not just in terms of what we do together but of *how* we do it and *who* we are together. We are better, not *despite* the attacks, the schemes, the busyness, or the difficulties but *because of* them.

To reiterate a salient point, perhaps the best thing you can do for your marriage while engaged in foster care is to not let it become all about foster care. Let Jesus *in your marriage* take precedence even over Jesus *in your mission*. I don't mean to imply that you're to abandon your mission for a self-centered pursuit of comfort and stability, but to emphasize the critical importance of building a firm foundation within your marriage—a basis upon which you can radically and sacrificially live out your God-given mission together longer, better and more effectively. The cyclical nature of marriage and mission is such that your marriage will fuel your mission, and in return your mission together will bring fulfillment, satisfaction, joy, and purpose to your marriage in deep and profound ways.

> **Satan wants the mission of foster care to break your marriage, but God has the capacity to build your marriage through it, if you'll allow Him to.**

PERSONAL REFLECTION

1. In what ways has your marriage experienced the weight of spiritual warfare? What have you done together to stand against the enemy attacks? How have you come out stronger because of your proactive stance?

2. In what ways has a "new version" of your spouse and of your marriage been revealed throughout the fostering journey? What specific qualities of your spouse have you come to better understand and more deeply appreciate during the course of the journey?

3. How successful have you been as a couple at refusing to allow your marriage to become defined by and consumed with foster care? In what ways can you grow in this pursuit? What priorities, behaviors, or rhythms need to change in order for you to protect your marriage?

GROUP DISCUSSION

1. What truth or idea stood out for you most vividly in this session? Why?

2. Whose idea was it initially to become foster parents? How long did it take for the two of you to be on the same page concerning the issue? Describe that process. How would you counsel another couple facing that same dilemma?

3. How has your engagement with foster care strengthened your marriage? What unique struggles have you endured because of its demands? What characteristics, positive

or negative, of your spouse have you seen through this process that you hadn't observed before, or what traits or qualities have you seen more fully demonstrated or developed on the basis of the fostering experience?

4. In what ways have you seen your marriage become a target for the enemy's attacks through your foster care journey? What practical tactics have you and your spouse implemented to ensure that your marriage doesn't become defined by and consumed with foster care?

PLAN OF ACTION

1. What specific perspectives, attitudes, or ways of thinking might need to change in order for you to more fully live out the ideas discussed in this section?

2. What specific actions or behaviors might need to change in order for you to more completely live out the ideas discussed in this section?

3. Based on what has been discussed in this section, complete the following statement as thoroughly and honestly as you can: *I will choose to honor God through this by . . .*

> *Being "married for a mission" can revitalize a lot*
> *of marriages in which partners think they suffer from*
> *a lack of compatibility; my suspicion is that many of*
> *these couples actually suffer from a lack of purpose.*
>
> GARY THOMAS

CHAPTER 11

FOSTER CARE AND WHAT I FEARED MOST FOR MY OWN KIDS

We were in the middle of building our new home. The process had been fun, especially since our daughters were old enough to enjoy it with us. They got excited about their new rooms, new neighborhood, and new friends next door and down the street.

The whole process resulted in several interesting conversations with them—most notably about how many more sisters they wanted in our family and where their rooms would be in the new house. We'd walk through the construction zone, when walls were nothing more than a skeleton grid of two-by-fours, pointing out different rooms along the way: This is a bathroom, a closet, your room, or the laundry room, whereupon they would ask, "But where's the new sister's room going to be? Where will she sleep?"

Even in the ceremonial practice of putting our hands in the wet cement of our newly poured driveway—six sets of handprints at the same time—the girls were concerned about how we would get a new sister's handprint into the concrete after it had dried! We assured them that we would find a way, even if it meant cutting out a square and pouring in new wet cement!

On some level they understood something just as fully as my wife and I did: that this house wasn't to be just for us— and that it was so much more than just a house.

The entire process gave us yet another small glimpse into something big that was happening in our family—and, more specifically, in our daughters. Foster care and adoption were changing us, not only in the obvious, family-picture kinds of ways but also in the more subtle, less apparent, and more perspective-shifting ways. Our daughters hadn't been unaffected—they wanted and expected more sisters—they wanted our home to be a place where kids who needed a family could find one, either for a little while or forever.

So do we.

A different kind of concern

My wife and I were initially concerned about the potentially negative effects that bringing foster children into our home might have had on our biological kids. Would it detract from the attention they deserve from us? Would it interrupt their routines? Would they resent us for having done it?

As I've shared earlier, now, after the fact, we've become more concerned about the effect NOT opening our home to foster care might have had on our kids. The experience, we see in hindsight, has changed them for the better—certainly not because everything has been easy but more likely because many aspects have been hard. We're convinced that they are better, stronger, and more mature because of it.

The norm of entitlement

The natural posture of parenting often bends itself toward protecting our kids at all costs. And rightly so in many ways—there's no shortage of dangers from which to guard them. However, if opening our home to foster care has taught us anything about being parents, it's that there's a fine line between protecting our kids from the dangers of being exposed to hard things and protecting them from the hazards inherent in NOT ever being exposed to them. My natural tendency would be to create an insular world of comfort and convenience for them, while unintentionally never allowing them to see and respond to the world of brokenness and hopelessness that exists all around them.

Yet, perhaps my greatest fear as a parent shouldn't be the dangers and difficulties that exist around my daughters but the self-centeredness and feelings of entitlement that can easily grow within them. Perhaps my primary goal as a dad shouldn't be to raise safe girls but to raise strong ones. If our society is characterized today by anything, it's self-indulgent, self-entitled kids. I see it in my own. That's the terrifying norm. Let's be abnormal.

A collision of two worlds

Foster care is nothing if not the collision of two worlds—one of relative ease and comfort is systematically dismantled so that ideally one of extreme brokenness and loss can have the opportunity to be restored. My daughters' worlds were changed the day their new sister became a part of them. Their worlds have also been changed through the grief of having to say goodbye. They've been altered through the trauma of having someone else's trauma significantly disrupt our home. My daughters have seen the police at our house because of foster care. They've seen their mom and dad hurt and struggle and cry because of foster care. They've sacrificed and questioned and loved in ways they might otherwise never have had to because of foster care. Their journey has by no means been easy, but they now know some important things about this world they did not know before: it's hard and broken and costly.

They sit in classrooms at school, go to gymnastics class and soccer practice, attend Sunday school, and have playdates with their friends on the weekends—all with a new and different normal from most of the other kids around them. They see a different world, and they see the world differently. Foster care has given them something we as Mom and Dad would likely never have been able to offer them on our own: perspective.

Would-be foster and adoptive parents have very real and oftentimes legitimate concerns over the effects that bringing a child from a hard place into their homes can have on their biological children. I'm not oblivious to that and don't negate the importance of this consideration. We've had to say no to some things because we just didn't feel the exposure to our family at that time would have been safe or wise. By no means am I suggesting that we compromise the safety of our children. But an equally legitimate concern we should have for our kids is the honest awareness that we as parents are prone to raise them in a sheltered, child-centered, entitlement-oriented environment—all in the name of their safety. This too is dangerous.

Raising the next generation of adults

It's sometimes easy to lose sight of the fact that we're currently raising the next generation of adults. In the blink of an eye our kids today will take their places as the adults of tomorrow. Compound that with the disturbing reality that when our kids are adults there will still be marginalized, abused, and vulnerable children in this world, and the question of who will be there to take care of them must both haunt and compel us. That reality is devastating for obvious reasons but motivating for others: it reminds us that, right now, today, we as moms and dads are raising the next generation of people who may themselves stand ready to care for kids from hard places tomorrow. While I certainly don't intend these remarks to be prescriptive—as though it's a given that your kids will take up the mantle of foster care or adoption as adults—there can be no doubt that the impact of growing up in a home that is oriented around that cause will be immeasurable in terms of its potential expression in the values and rhythms of life your kids will establish for themselves in the future.

My wife and I certainly aren't perfect parents, nor are we raising perfect kids. We continually wrestle with wanting to provide for our girls without creating a sense of entitlement in them. Like most parents we don't always know or understand the implications of what we're doing, but I do know one thing: our daughters often talk about wanting more sisters and push us to say yes to hard things even when as mom and dad we're ready for things to just be "easy" for a while. As a father my heart rejoices when I hear them express their hearts in that way. I hear them saying *There's more to be done—the work isn't over, and more kids need to know they're loved.*

So there will indefinitely be space in our home, and if nothing else, in our hearts, for just that.

I fear for our daughters if there isn't.

" There's a fine line between protecting our kids from the dangers of being exposed to hard things and protecting them from the hazards inherent in NOT ever being exposed to them.

PERSONAL REFLECTION

1. Was there something in your childhood you can cite as an influence with regard to your adult decision to involve yourself in foster care? A specific person, place, or event? How did this impetus plant something in your heart as a kid that prodded you to move in this direction? In what other areas of life have you seen God use past experiences to influence present decisions?

2. How have you seen God at work in your child's life as a result of your opening your home to foster care? How has foster care helped create an environment for your biological children today that will potentially influence them for years to come?

3. How would you counsel your best friends if they were hesitant to get involved in foster care because of apprehension over how it might affect their biological kids?

GROUP DISCUSSION

1. What truth or idea stood out for you most strongly in this session? Why?

2. How would you counsel your best friends if they were hesitant to get involved in foster care because of how it might affect their biological kids? If anyone in the group is still processing through that concern, allow them time to share and discuss.

3. In what practical ways do you involve your biological children in the foster care process? How do you

protect your kids from the possibility of their being "overshadowed" by a foster placement or feeling resentful for the time and attention the new child needs and deserves? How have you seen God change your children as a result of opening your home to foster care?

4. Was there something in your childhood that you would say was an influence on your decision as an adult to get involved in foster care? A specific person, place or event? How did it plant something in your heart as a kid that influenced your decision to get involved in foster care today?

PLAN OF ACTION

1. What specific perspectives, attitudes, or ways of thinking might need to change in order for you to more effectively live out the ideas discussed in this section?

2. What specific actions or behaviors might need to change in order to enhance your ability to live out the ideas discussed in this section?

3. Based on what has been discussed in this section, complete the following statement as thoroughly and honestly as you can: *I will choose to honor God through this by* ...

The ultimate purpose of parenting is not to hang on, but to let go; not protection but empowerment.

J. D. GREEAR

It was a Friday evening in early October the first time the phone rang for a placement. My parents had been certified for foster care only three hours earlier, following months of preparation and training. I was seven at the time, listening in from the other room as my mom scribbled down details on an old scrap of paper:

> *3-month-old girl.*
> *12 fractured bones.*
> *Placement needed immediately.*

Soon afterward she was dropped off at our home, and life as I knew it permanently changed.

I walked over to the couch where she sat quietly in her car seat. Her legs were tightly secured in casts, and her big brown eyes stared back at me, uncertain and afraid. I can only imagine that my own eyes reflected similarly—though based on a different kind of fear. The first time I held her, her broken ribs popped so loudly I quickly handed her back to my mom.

Prior to this event my childhood had been easy, predictable, and protected. I was the youngest of four daughters, and our days were spent reading beside the fireplace; running barefoot with friends through our safe, suburban neighborhood; attending piano lessons; and playing with dolls in the attic. No part of the first seven years of my life had provided the context or space for me to understand abuse and neglect—and I'm grateful for that. But on this first day of our being a licensed foster family there was no way my parents could explain away a visibly abused infant.

My questions were incessant and many: *How did this happen? Who did it? Why would someone hurt a baby?*

My parents answered honestly and openly. I didn't have the language or development to grasp the weightiness of what I was seeing, but years later I began to understand that those initial questions and confusion, along with my heart's pull for justice, had planted a seed that would impact the entirety of my life.

Over the next ten years my framework for understanding the world was uniquely established through the lens of foster care. I first learned about drugs when I heard the cries of an infant going through withdrawal, and the concepts of homelessness, robbery, and incarceration were introduced as siblings arrived bearing those specific scars and carrying those backstories. My mom made an intentional decision for me and my sisters to spend time in the office when she was transporting kids to visits; she wanted us to see that behind each child we cared for were parents and families doing the best they could with their circumstances. During those visits I saw how birth families doted on their babies, just as ours doted on them at home; I came to understand that a parent's love transcends even the harshest of barriers. I also saw the depth of hurt attached to a humanity that is victim to generational poverty and trauma.

There were days when questions came faster than my parents could provide answers. Siblings came and left, and my heart knew frequent aches. By nature I am a deep feeler, so each goodbye was profoundly felt.

In the middle of my senior year of high school my parents adopted my two youngest sisters. The outcome of their case had been in limbo for several years, and I saw additional, avoidable hurts on the basis of the delays. I grew angry. During those months of uncertainty, foster care was transformed for me from a family experience in which I participated by default to a missional cause that was personal, intentional, and intimate. A desire to preserve families and fight for the well-being of kids became my life purpose. How could I dare pretend to unsee the faces and stories of the kids who had accompanied so much of my childhood? I no longer had the luxury of not knowing. I ultimately chose to pursue my bachelors and masters degrees in social work, and through all the other challenges that accompanied young adulthood I never once questioned my profession. My experiences had solidified an unquestionable and unquenchable purpose.

Years after our own foster home was "closed," I asked my mom what it was like watching her children grieve after the eventual departure of each placement. She shared with me that there had been times when she'd questioned whether it was right to intentionally allow avoidable pain to lie in the paths of her kids. Her resolve was this: "There is nothing we can do to protect our kids from pain and suffering, and it's better to experience that inevitable pain doing something God has clearly asked us to do than to experience the pain and suffering that come from disobedience."

That sentiment grounds me on my hardest days even now. The faces and stories of the kids I once called my sisters and brothers are with me each day at work. Our shared experiences are my drive to be a better social worker and advocate. Even while holding remnants of grief, I look back on my childhood and am deeply grateful that my parents chose for our family to be one that opened our hearts a little bit wider to the "least of these."

Kylee Craggett, LMSW
grew up with foster and adoptive siblings;
currently working to license and support
kinship families in Dallas, TX

CHAPTER 12

FOR THE HUSBAND WHO ISN'T SURE

It was only a few years ago. We had three young daughters, a new church plant, and a conversation one night that would forever change the course of our family.

She was ready for us to become foster parents. I was not.

It had been an ongoing discussion for months. A very cordial one, at that. We were reading the same book of "God is calling us to this," we just weren't quite on the same page yet. While I had been delaying the move forward in the name of it "not being the right time," she had become prayerfully convinced that it was. The conversation that day was a carbon copy of the many other discussions we'd had had on the subject up to that point. She firmly believed that now was the time. I outlined all the reasons I thought it wasn't. She patiently listened. That was it for now, . . . or so I thought.

Later that evening, though, she brought it up again. Something in her voice told me that this time was different from all the others. Not that the dialogue hadn't been serious before, but the tone was different—a new urgency and straightforwardness wrapped around this moment—through which she said the one thing I secretly knew to be true but selfishly hoped I would never have to confront:

"There will never be a right time for us to do this; there will always be a reason not to. There are kids out there who need us. The time is now."

I don't recall much of what was said after that, if anything at all. I do remember, however, knowing that she was right. She went upstairs and left me in the silent wake of her words. A few minutes later I followed.

A broken leader

God changed my heart that night, in more ways than one. I have always wanted to be a husband who led his wife well. I grew up in a church tradition teaching that men are designed to lead their wives and are responsible to use their positions of leadership not in order to be served but to serve—to sacrifice themselves for the good of their brides. This is the model of Jesus, and it's the means by which I've always strived to love and lead my wife.

But leading can be hard. Up to that point in our marriage I had found the most difficult part of leading my wife not to have been making big decisions, being on the spiritual frontlines in defense of our marriage and family, managing money, or even working hard to provide a home. Instead, I found that being the spiritual leader in my marriage was always most difficult for me when I sensed that my wife was more spiritually capable of leading than I was. Who was I, a broken and flawed man, to pretend I could lead her?

How was I supposed to model the leadership of Jesus for my wife when it seemed as though she was walking more closely with Him than I was? It felt most difficult and awkward for me as a husband to lead my wife when she wanted to be led by God and I didn't . . . until that night.

When leading means following

One of the great misconceptions about leadership is that a leader always has to be out front, when in fact some of the best leaders I've known have at times been the least visible people in the room. They inspire, empower, and steward others to flourish in the things they do well—even if they themselves are less than capable of effectively doing those things. That's what makes them leaders.

When it comes to my marriage, I have realized that there will indeed be times when leading my wife means stepping out in front of her, . . . *and* there will be times when it means being willing to step behind and follow her—trusting her to step out in front in order to create space for me to catch up. I don't think that makes me a bad leader; I think it makes me a smart one. On some level I'm convinced that this is what Scripture has in mind when it describes the wife as a "helper" for her husband (Genesis 2:18). Sometimes, as a man, a husband, and a leader, I need help.

Most of the time, in fact. But I suppose that's the beauty of how marriage is designed to work: as a mutual sharing of the burden to help each other continue to take steps forward, in harmony, together. Sometimes I can lead well in the traditional sense of the term, and at other times I need her to take the first step so I can see more clearly where we both need to go together.

On that night in particular, leading her meant literally following her—upstairs to tell her she was right . . . because she was. It was time.

I know this isn't the story of every marriage—some couples, for example, are totally in sync on all points; some have real, hard reasons for why now *isn't* the right time; and in others it's the wife, not the husband, who has hesitations. But it was the story of mine and, I'm convinced, the current reality of many others. Maybe including yours.

To the uncertain husband

Husbands, God may not speak audibly, but I'm convinced that He does speak vicariously—and never more clearly than through our wives. For me, it was most profound that night: *There will never be a right time for us to do this; there will always be a reason not to. But there are kids out there who need us. The time is now.* She was right. And the truth is that there's never really a perfect time to foster or adopt; just a lot of opportunities to say yes despite the many reasons we may have to say no. You're aware of all the reasons you have to say no, but perhaps God is using the voice of your wife to help you say yes to His. He certainly did for me.

Some will say, "It's important that both the husband and wife feel called," and I would whole-heartedly agree. That is, after all, the point—perhaps God is making that call very clear to you through your wife. It's in those cases that leading your wife well will mean trusting what God's put on her heart—like fostering or adopting—and following her into it, together. I mentioned early on that my wife and I were "reading the same book" but weren't quite on the same page yet. Here's what I mean by that — we both knew there was a foster care crisis, that God cared deeply about it and that we should probably do something about it. We were reading the same book. She was just several pages ahead of me! That meant she needed to slow down a bit, and I needed to speed up a bit and start taking some steps forward . . . and eventually we met in the same place.

Maybe it starts small and simple; one step at a time. Attending an informational meeting at church or an orientation class at a local agency; going to dinner with a family that is fostering or has adopted to hear their story and ask them questions; reading a book or attending a conference. Such relatively small, investigative steps could go a long way towards encouraging the heart of your wife and potentially doing a big work in yours.

I want to encourage you to be free from the odd expectation to always be on the "same page" before moving forward. If that were the requirement with everything we'd likely never really do anything. Marriage requires trust, and an ability and willingness to slow down on one end and speed up on the other so that eventually you can end up on the same page, even while the whole time you've been reading the same book. This is when we say to one another, "I'm not 100% as sure as you are, but I trust you and am willing to follow, learn and grow."

Husbands, lead well in whatever that next step may be. For now this may feel more like following, but I'm convinced that God wants to use your wife's leading to change your heart in ways you might never before have imagined. Perhaps she is the very help God knew you would need to become the husband He knew she would need.

" Husbands, God may not speak audibly, but I'm convinced that He does speak vicariously—and never more clearly than through our wives.

PERSONAL REFLECTION

1. Husbands, if you were to narrow down your reasons for hesitation to one specific underlying concern, what would it be? If you were sitting across the table from God sharing that objection with Him, what do you think He would say in response?

2. How did God help move you beyond that no, and what has He shown you as a result? If you haven't yet finalized your decision, what circumstances would need to be in place in your life in order for you to finally say yes? How would you assess the realistic likelihood of those circumstances ever fully coming to pass?

3. What have you learned about being a leader in your home and marriage throughout this process?

GROUP DISCUSSION

1. What truth or idea stood out to you most in this session? Why?

2. In what other areas of your life have you said no to something only to have eventually, and perhaps reluctantly, substituted a yes? Explain.

3. What factors would have to change in order for you to turn your specific no into a yes, or perhaps even into just a "maybe, but I need to learn more"? What steps can you begin taking (or continue taking) in the direction of changing some of those factors?

4. What role do (or did) you allow your spouse, friends, or outside community of support to play in helping you move beyond some of your reasons for hesitation?

PLAN OF ACTION

1. What specific perspectives, attitudes, or ways of thinking might need to change in order for you to more fully live out the ideas discussed in this section?

2. What specific actions or behaviors might need to change in order for you to more effectively live out the ideas discussed in this section?

3. Based on what has been discussed in this section, complete the following statement as thoroughly and honestly as you can: *I will choose to honor God through this by . . .*

Men, you'll never be a good groom to your wife
unless you're first a good bride to Jesus.

TIM KELLER

CHAPTER 13

LOVING A CHILD WHO MIGHT LEAVE

I'll never forget the day it all changed for me. Like so many others who are considering venturing down the beautiful yet tumultuous path of foster care, my greatest fear wasn't whether I could love a child who wasn't my own but whether or not I could handle letting go of a child I had grown to love as my own.

I couldn't get beyond this concern and found myself unable to move forward because of it. I shared my fear with a friend who was a foster dad at the time, and his response both challenged and settled me. He gently revealed that I had it backward—that my concerns were centered on me and how I *might* feel rather than on the children and how they *do* feel.

He shared that he and his wife were committed to experiencing the pain of loving a child they might lose if this meant that a child who had lost so much could experience the gain of their love. A new and profound concept for me at the time, but one filled with a purity and simplicity that respostured my concern—away from what I stood to lose in the direction of what a child might stand to gain. In the simplest of terms I realized that it truly isn't about me—it's about these kids.

A different kind of fear

As my wife and I began our foster care journey with a three-day-old baby girl, we had to make the same decision for ourselves: that we would rather experience the pain of a profound personal loss if it meant that this little girl placed in our home, and any others to follow, could experience the gain of a deep love—no matter how long they stayed with us. We would embrace the heartache of having to let them go if it meant that they had known, if even for a short time, what it means to truly be held on to. We resolved not to let our fear of loving a child who might leave deter us but to allow the fear of a child never knowing our love to drive us. This is a very different kind of fear—a hard one, indeed, but I'm convinced a better one.

Most foster parents have heard some variation of the classic *I don't know if I could fully love a child knowing I might have to let them go* rebuttal, and every foster parent has had to wrestle with the weight of that statement in their own heart and mind. This is an inherent tension that comes with loving a child who isn't your own—a tension that often deters people in fear from getting involved.

We all understand that the end goal of foster care is to provide safe and loving permanence for a child, and we also know that "permanence" for them might not mean permanence for us. Our motivations are severely challenged by the very real possibility of such a personal loss, often exposing within us a posture that is more concerned about what it will cost us to give love to a child than what it will cost a child to never have received love from us. Yet, as we weigh what we stand to lose against what they stand to gain, the answer is simple—though hardly easy: we can't let the fear of loving a child that might leave deter us; we must let the fear of a child never knowing our love drive us.

Giving our family for a child

Foster care is less about getting a child for your family and more about giving your family for a child—again, an only slightly different statement with significantly different implications. Our first responsibility is to give, not to receive; to open our family to a child whose world would otherwise be closed off to the safety and security of knowing a nurturing and loving home.

That isn't to say that a family can't grow numerically through foster care—the process sometimes does lead to adoption—or receive through it endless amounts of blessing and joy. It *is* to say, however, that our first call is to give, not to receive—to recognize that true and effective service for others almost always involves full sacrifice of self.

Foster care and the gospel

The gospel implications bear repeating here: In the end, our call is to fully love these children while we have them and to accept the costs we may incur as worthwhile in terms of the gain they stand to receive. This is in essence what Jesus has done for us: He joyfully laid down the infinite value of His own life so that we might know the immeasurable worth of being fully and unconditionally loved in Him. Foster care, as we've observed earlier, is a beautiful expression of the gospel. It demands a selfless, costly, and potentially painful love for the sake of a child gaining much as we willingly give all. As we labor to love with the love we ourselves have received from Jesus, we do so from within a cloud of uncertainties and unknowns, but with the confidence of one guarantee: it's worth it.

By no means do I want to diminish the very real and raw stories of families who have loved someone else's child as their own and after eight days or eighteen months or even several years been required to let them go. We have felt that grief deeply along with you—a pain that will always feel visceral when revisited and will never fully go away.

One particular night has forever been seared into the collective consciousness of our family. Emma (name changed for privacy) was a beautiful eight-year-old girl staying with us. She fit our family well, and we loved her deeply. Even in her short time with us we had begun developing a long-term vision for what our family might look like with her as a forever part of it. But everything changed unexpectedly (which could aptly be the tagline for this type of ministry: "Foster Care: Everything Changed Unexpectedly").

That day hadn't been unlike any other: she had headed off to school with our other daughters with plans to come home, play outside, and attend a theater performance that evening featuring one of our other daughters. Shortly after lunch I received a call from our agency, however, notifying us that Emma would be leaving that night. Our agency director was confused. We were shocked, and after contacting multiple people at the state office we learned that a closed-door deal had been made among caseworkers, lawyers, and the judge earlier that day. The decree was issued to place her near her birth home with a family friend—a nonrelative with whom she was moderately familiar—someone who lived so close to her home that many of the dangers to which she had been exposed might all too easily have direct access to her once again. We knew this wasn't right and dreaded the conversation that was to come a few hours later when she returned home from school.

She bounded off the bus and immediately grabbed a scooter to play outside. She'd had a great day—meeting new friends and settling into her new rhythm of life. Our hearts ached for what was to come, not because of how difficult her leaving would be for us but because of how crushing we knew it would be for her. She had to leave, we had to break the news to her, and there was nothing we could do to stop it.

As expected, she wept. And so did we.

There's nothing quite like putting a little girl for whom you've developed a deep love into the back of a caseworker's car, knowing without a doubt that her new destination wouldn't be good or safe for her—even amidst her tears and despite her *begging* us not to make her leave:

"Please don't make me go. I don't want to leave."

We don't want you to either, sweetheart. With everything inside of us, we want you here.

This kind of scenario is gut-wrenching, frustrating, devastating, and yet, we must firmly believe, never without ultimate meaning and purpose. The stories of others who've had similar moments branded into their souls consistently on some level sound the same, ending with the acknowledgment that while it was devastating to let them go it had been worth it to have had the opportunity to love them. Hard? Yes. Worth it? No question.

For further reading check out "Five Things to Know About the Fear of Getting Too Attached" on www.jasonjohnsonblog.com.

" We can't let the fear of loving a child that might leave deter us; we must let the fear of a child never knowing our love drive us.

PERSONAL REFLECTION

1. How have you processed this very real tension every foster parent (or prospective foster parent) faces? Even in the face of likely heartache, what compels you to continue to engage in fostering?

2. If you have grieved the process of loving a child and letting go, in what ways did you experience the mercy and comfort of God through that heartwrenching time? How has He been uniquely merciful to you through this very difficult aspect of fostering? Looking back, do you consider the experience to have been "worth it" for you and your family? Why and in what ways?

3. What particular aspect of the gospel has been made most acutely relevant to you throughout this journey of loving and letting go?

GROUP DISCUSSION

1. What truth or idea stood out for you most intensely in this session? Why?

2. If anyone in the group has walked through the grief of loving a child and having had to let go, have them briefly share their experience. What did you learn through the process? What in particular helped you heal and move forward? If anyone in the group is considering fostering but is concerned about "getting too attached," give them space to share those fears and process them openly within a safe community of caring people.

3. How would you counsel your best friends if their reason for not becoming foster parents was apprehension about "getting too attached"?

4. Throughout this resource we are working to reframe some of our experiences and perceptions of the fostering journey. How does the gospel most practically help us reframe this particular reality of fostering? What aspects of the gospel are most crucial for us to hold on to in the midst of this "loving and letting go" tension? Explain.

PLAN OF ACTION

1. What specific perspectives, attitudes, or ways of thinking might need to change in order for you to more easily live out the ideas discussed in this section?

2. What specific actions or behaviors might need to change in order for you to more effectively live out the ideas discussed in this section?

3. Based on what has been discussed in this section, complete the following statement as thoroughly and honestly as you can: *I will choose to honor God through this by . . .*

You don't really know Jesus is all you need until Jesus is all you have.

TIM KELLER

CHAPTER 14

THE SOVEREIGNTY OF GOD IN FOSTER CARE

I'll never forget one particular night very early on in our fostering journey. As I rocked someone else's baby girl to sleep—a little girl for whom I had quickly developed a deep love—the reality of our future with her hit me. The truth that she might not live with us forever had always been top of mind, but as I looked around her room that night—taking in her crib, her dresser, her folded pile of pjs and blankets on the nightstand—it became all the more real that this might not be her room for much longer. One day soon she might have a very different room.

While we rocked back and forth as the calm of the night filled the room, I found myself compelled to do battle with the competing hopes that had begun filling my heart. On the one hand I wanted to keep her forever, while on the other I was praying and even hoping that her mom would find stability and health and be ready before long to bring her baby girl back home—two very different hopes that couldn't simultaneously materialize. We would be thrilled to keep her, but devastated by all that would need to be lost in order for that to happen. This is the great juxtaposition of foster care—learning to love tightly and hold loosely.

I realized something that had always been true but was finally made clear to me that night in the quiet, darkened nursery: there were no guarantees that she could stay with us, grow up with our daughters as her big sisters, walk to school with us on her first day of kindergarten, celebrate losing her first tooth with us, learn how to drive with me next to her, launch off to college from the security of our home or walk down the aisle on her wedding day with me by her side. None of these things were guaranteed us. And that lack of a guarantee was inevitable and necessary.

We hoped and prayed for these things, and we loved her then as though those future dreams would one day materialize for us, but there were no guarantees that she would ever know how much we had grown to love her or how desperately we longed for her to become a part of us forever. If we really wanted to love her the way she needed, all of that had to be okay too.

Our one guarantee

In fostering this precious girl, and others to come along the way, we had to choose the pain of possibly losing her if it meant that she had gained the benefits of us having had her— for however long or short we were privileged to. We must willingly embrace the sting of a potentially devastating loss if it meant that she could know the kisses of a very great love.

While we mourned the certain possibility that she may be removed from our home, we had to accept the joyous privilege of giving all of ourselves to her while she was here. In the end, that is the reality of foster care—not *getting* a child for your family but *giving* your family for a child and willingly embracing whatever implications might come along the way.

We understood the possibilities of what could—and most likely would—come, yet spoke very little about them. Much was communicated in our silence; most of the time the looming truth was too tense to invite conversation. We almost felt that if we ignored that reality long enough the likelihood of her leaving would somehow decrease.

I knew we could provide her a good home, a safe and loving environment, and possibilities and opportunities that might not otherwise become available to her. She would be loved, cared for, and protected in our home with every ounce of our energy. Yet for all we may have been able to provide, if the day came when she did need to leave, my only hope would reside in the fact that God's ability to be good to her even in a difficult environment remained infinitely greater than any good we could have offered her in our comfortable one.

No amount of "good" from our side could have begun to compare to the goodness of the sovereign and all-loving God in her life, wherever she might end up living it.

There are no guarantees in foster care, except one (and this makes all the difference): God is sovereign in the lives of these kids. He *is* good and *will be* good to them always, no matter where they might lay their heads at night.

I realized that night, at the very outset of our fostering journey, that I very likely wasn't going to be able to love and care for any of these kids through all the unknowns and uncertainties without a growing dependency upon the sovereignty of God in all things. If He were not in control of it all, I don't see how there could be any hope in it at all. His sovereignty is my sanity. It's all I have to hold on to much of the time. Colossians 1:16-17 says this of Jesus: *"All things were created through Him and for Him. He is before all things, and in Him all things hold together."* He holds ALL things together — these kids, these families, this journey . . . and us. His sovereignty over all is our sanity through all.

Foster care and the gospel

Foster care is a beautiful expression of the gospel. It demands a selfless, costly, and potentially painful love for the sake of a child's gaining much as we willingly give all. As we labor to love these kids with the love we ourselves have received from Jesus, we do so in a cloud of uncertainties and unknowns, but with the confidence of one guarantee: that God's sovereignty in their lives is for their good—both now and always.

We rock them to sleep each night with this certain hope.

> **Foster care is a beautiful expression of the gospel. It demands a selfless, costly, and potentially painful love for the sake of a child's gaining much as we willingly give all.**

PERSONAL REFLECTION

1. How has the sovereignty of God over all things shown itself to be true in your own life? In what specific ways have you seen His faithfulness through an especially uncertain or trying season or circumstance?

2. Why is it important to trust in God's sovereignty over the lives of these kids? What effect does this trust have on you as a foster parent? How difficult would it be for you to cope if you lacked the assurance of His love and providence, both in their lives and in your own?

3. In what specific ways are you struggling to fully internalize your belief that God is in control over all the circumstances of your foster children's lives, their legal cases, and their future paths? What steps can you take to resolve this issue? What aspects of the gospel have been most relevant to you as you labor to love these kids with the love you have received from Jesus "within a cloud of uncertainties and unknowns."

GROUP DISCUSSION

1. What truth or idea stood out to you most intensely in this session? Why?

2. Have you personally grappled with the "competing hopes" of wanting a child to stay but also wanting to see a birth family become healthy, restored, and intact? How have you processed this seeming contradiction? How has your assurance of the sovereignty of God

helped you navigate some of the unique nuances and difficulties that come along the journey of fostering?

3.   In what ways has foster care forced you to relinquish any sense of control? How has it forced you to increasingly lean into the sovereignty of God, not just in fostering but in other areas and aspects of your life as well?

4.   How would you counsel your best friends with regard to how to prepare to wrestle with these "competing hopes"? What would you say to encourage those who are experiencing that tension now?

PLAN OF ACTION

1.   What specific perspectives, attitudes, or ways of thinking might need to change in order for you to more consistently live out the ideas discussed in this section?

2.   What specific actions or behaviors might need to change in order for you to better live out the ideas discussed in this section?

3.   Based on what has been discussed in this section, complete the following statement as thoroughly and honestly as you can: *I will choose to honor God through this by . . .*

> *There is not a square inch in the whole domain*
> *of our human existence over which Christ,*
> *who is Sovereign over all, does not cry, "Mine!"*
>
> ABRAHAM KUYPER

CHAPTER 15

FOSTER CARE: A FAMILY-GIVING MECHANISM

I've said it before, but the principle more than bears repeating: foster care is less about getting a child for your family and more about giving your family for a child. Caring for vulnerable children doesn't hinge upon what we might get out of the experience but upon what we're called to give into it, no matter what.

Of all the gifts we can give a child in foster care, none is more precious than the safety and security of a loving family. The lack of safety and security is what ushers children in the first place into the vulnerable situations in which they find themselves, so providing these things for them is paramount. No longer without the care and nurturing they once lacked, they now know experientially that these things exist in the real world—not just in words spoken to them but through the encircling arms of those who have willingly, joyfully, and sacrificially done what was necessary to afford them the safety and security of a family who would love them as their own.

A family-giving mechanism

Foster care, then, is a family-giving mechanism before it is a family-growth mechanism. It's the call to open your home and family to a child whose world would otherwise be closed to the security of knowing nurture and love. To reiterate, that isn't to say that your family can't grow numerically through foster care—it very well might through adoption—or that you won't collectively receive endless amounts of blessing and joy in the process—you undoubtedly will. It *is* to say that your first call is to give, not to receive—to recognize that true service of others always involves true sacrifice of self.

It's often the case that we go into foster care with a desire to give but then quickly have our motives confronted and severely tested when what we're getting in return is inconvenient, difficult, or below the level of our expectation. We all know that the process is often laborious and overwhelming, involving as it does the "extra" output involved with juggling paperwork, finances, home inspections, court hearings, lawyers, and the endless red-tape of government agencies. These requirements, and many others like them, will readily expose any "What's in it for me?" attitudes and force us to deal with them in one of two ways—either by resenting it or by repenting of it. They will also force us to repeatedly ask and answer a vitally important question: *Why are we doing this?*

The beauty of the gospel is found in that space between "this is what we hoped for" and "this isn't at all what we signed up for." The mercy of God fills that chasm, and reminds us that the work is worth it. A child deserves to know what it's like to be raised in a loving and caring home. A child needs the family you have right now and is dependent upon your willingness to do whatever it takes to provide it.

When the line blurs

As we began the process of fostering, our assumptions were pretty simple: we would bring a child into our family. Unexpectedly, however, something profound began to happen. The line began to blur to the point that we weren't quite sure whether we were bringing a little girl into our family or she was drawing our family into herself. Again, a subtle distinction with significantly different implications:

- It wasn't about what we could get but about what she needed—and, in some way, even demanded—us to give.
- It wasn't about what it cost us but about what the whole experience might gain for her.
- In the simplest, most brutally honest terms possible, it wasn't about us at all but solely about her.

The gospel in foster care

The gospel is by nature rooted in the act of giving. It's the story of God's great exchange for our infinite gain. He laid down the inestimable value of His own life in Jesus so that we might know the immeasurable worth of being fully loved in Him (2 Corinthians 8:9). We were in need, so He gave His one and only Son (John 3:16). Giving is at the heart of the gospel because giving is God's heart. It's just who He is and what He does, over and over and over again. This is the essence of the gospel and the platform upon which we approach foster care.

In the end, we give our families to these kids and willingly embrace any and all implications that come to us as a result. We give so they might gain. This is exactly what Jesus has done for us in the gospel and is paramount in the posture we take toward the work of bringing a child into our family—and the even greater honor we have of bringing our family to a child.

" Foster care is less about getting a child for your family and more about giving your family for a child.

PERSONAL REFLECTION

1. Why is it important to understand the distinction between "getting a child for our family" and "giving our family for a child"? On the spectrum of "giving our family" vs. "getting a child," in which direction does your heart lean right now? Why?

2. Consider the implications of approaching foster care with a "getting a child" mentality. How might this play out when you don't feel as though you're getting what you want—or even what you "bargained for"—from the process? What happens when things get difficult and confusing? Now consider the implications of approaching foster care from a "family-giving" posture. How might this paradigm shift influence you when things get hard and the outcome is unclear? What implications does this have for your attitude toward birth parents?

3. What particular aspects of the gospel are most helpful for you to remember as you seek to walk out your fostering journey from a posture of "giving" rather than of "getting"?

GROUP DISCUSSION

1. What truth or idea stood out to you most clearly in this session? Why?

2. Discuss the implications of taking a "getting a child" stance in terms of your attitude toward foster care. How does this play out when you don't feel as though you're getting what we want from the process? What happens when things get difficult and confusing? Discuss the implications of having a "family-giving" posture towards foster care. How does this influence us when things get hard and the outcome is unclear? What implications does this have on our posture towards birth parents?

3. How have you personally experienced the implications of this distinction between "giving a family" and "getting a child" in your fostering journey? What tensions did you need to walk through? What freedoms have you found as a result of coming to grips with the validity of the "giving a child" perspective?

4. If you were to counsel someone just beginning their fostering journey, of what potential pitfalls would you warn them with regard to a "getting a child" approach? What benefits would you tell them come with taking a "giving your family" posture?

PLAN OF ACTION

1. What specific perspectives, attitudes, or ways of thinking might need to change in order for you to more meaningfully live out the ideas discussed in this section?

2. What specific actions or behaviors might need to change in order for you to more effectively live out the ideas discussed in this section?

3. Based on what has been discussed in this section, complete the following statement as thoroughly and honestly as you can: *I will choose to honor God through this by . . .*

*God has a way of giving by the cartloads to those
who give away by the shovelfuls.*

CHARLES SPURGEON

STORY

My husband and I had been foster parents for almost two years, caring for and then saying goodbye to six children before two little ones came to us who would eventually become our own. They came as a foster placement: a three-and-a-half-year-old girl and a sixteen-month-old boy. A short three months after they arrived parental rights were terminated, and we were adopting!

What a bittersweet feeling. We loved these little ones and were delighted to become their parents. However, their joining our family entailed for them the dismantling of another family, the first family my children had loved.

Everything happened so fast, causing our daughter to struggle deeply in terms of understanding what was going on. In her mind she had been kidnapped from the only family she had ever known and was now being told that she wouldn't be able to go back. She was understandably sad and homesick, grieving not only her family but also her favorite possessions. She would wistfully reflect, "If only I had known I wasn't going back, I would've brought my Hello Kitty microphone (or my new blanket and pillow)."

It's devastating to see a child grieve even the small things. Despite all the new possessions she had in her new life with us, she longed for that Hello Kitty microphone. I wished so much that we could get some of those things from her family of origin but knew that this wouldn't be feasible. The circumstances just wouldn't allow such an exchange at the time.

Due to the case moving forward so quickly, we had never actually met the children's biological family. However, our children's attorney had strongly suggested that we get in contact with their biological grandma because she loved them very much, even though she wasn't able to care for them.

My husband and I were reluctant for all the reasons you would expect. "Is this safe?" we worried. "Will this be more harmful than helpful for the kids?"

Selfishly, I wanted to keep my daughter and son to myself. I didn't want to compete for their affection with their biological family. We worried about the effect of such a visit on the hardwon progress in attachment we had made, but after a great deal of prayer and discussion we decided to attempt building a relationship with Grandma by sending an email. The process went better than we could ever have imagined! She was so wonderful in her correspondence with us that after a couple of months we moved on to phone calls with the kids, and finally to our first in-person visit, for which we established clear boundaries that were agreed upon by everyone.

Our initial visit was perfect. Upon meeting us, the children's grandmother hugged us all. She told my husband and me how much she loved us and appreciated how well we were loving her grandkids. This was almost too good to be true: visiting with her wasn't only easy but enjoyable!

About six months later she attended our daughter's birthday party. She brought along several gifts, one of which took my breath away: the cherished Hello Kitty microphone! Our daughter's grandmother understood all that she had lost and was able to restore this one item.

It was amazing for us to glimpse this picture of how deeply God cares for us—so profoundly that He wants to give us good gifts and satisfy the desires of our hearts, even when what we most desire is a Hello Kitty microphone.

We are two years into this open adoption journey, and I can honestly say that it has been the best experience of my life. We now have an open relationship with most of our children's biological family, including their birth mom and a biological sibling. In all honesty, our visits often feel weird and awkward, but there's something beautiful in them that I can't put into words.

I hate the thought of everything we would have missed had we not risked stepping out in faith.

Elizabeth Carter
Wife to Matthew, Mom to Reese and Rowan,
Foster and Adoptive Mom

CHAPTER 16

HOW FOSTER CARE PREACHES THE GOSPEL AND WHY WE MUST LET IT

We had settled into our seats in the mall food court when out of the corner of my eye I noticed it happening again. Her eyes bounced from my daughter to me, then back to my daughter, then back to me, each time causing her brow to wrinkle in greater curiosity and her mind to visibly race with more questions.

I had seen it happen a hundred times and knew exactly what she was thinking: *Is that her dad? Is she his daughter? He's white. She's, well—not really. He's bald. Her hair is big and wildly out of control. What's going on here? What's the story?*

I half-smiled at her and answered the question I knew she was waiting for permission to ask: "Yes, she's my daughter" and, in an attempt to diffuse the curiosity with humor, "Don't you see the resemblance?" With that the confused stranger next to us laughed with a sense of relief—a nd leaned in closer. Her curiosity was evident. The opportunity I was being given was apparent.

Our conversation naturally led to adoption and foster care and the big reason this precious little girl was now a part of our family—namely the heart of God demonstrated through the work of Jesus on our behalf in the gospel. She then offered a harmless attempt to be encouraging and supportive: "She's so lucky to have you."

I had heard things like that many times before so was fully prepared to respond in a way that was affirming but also slightly perspective-shifting for her: "It's funny how it feels like it's so much the other way around. We didn't anticipate it being like this going into it but have since realized how much *we're* the lucky ones by having her in our lives. She's opened our eyes to see things we could never have seen on our own, our hearts to feel things we could never have felt on our own, and our minds to understand things we could never have understood on our own. We're certainly the blessed ones here. Our family is better because of her."

She continued, "People like you are so special. I could never do that."

Again I responded: "We used to think the exact same thing—that only 'special' people could do this. We're just regular, normal people, and this seems like a very special thing for a special type of person. How could we do something that seems to require so much more than we think we have to give? We had to finally come to a place where we realized that it's less about what we think we can do, and our natural inclination to avoid hard and inconvenient things, and more about what we know God wants us to do, even if it's hard and inconvenient. We've learned that if ordinary people like us can do it, anybody could!"

Even after my extensive ramblings, she STILL continued, "I would love to do that, but I'm afraid I would just get too attached and wouldn't want to let them go." This statement is probably my favorite to answer—which I did, as follows:

"That's a valid concern, but one that most people tend to think backward about. Instead of letting the fear of getting too attached deter us, we should actually let the fear of these kids never feeling truly attached to someone drive us. These kids need people who are willing to love them enough to hurt for them if they ever have to let them go. If you know you'll get attached that likely means you'd be a fantastic foster parent. That's exactly what they need from you. And, in the end, is there really such a thing as getting 'too' attached? Probably not for the sake of these kids."

In this casual, unassuming place—the mall food court— the pulpit of adoption preached the power of the gospel to a curious onlooker. She heard about God's pursuit of her, the lengths He has gone to get her, and the unconditional love He has for her—all through the pulpit that foster care and adoption had constructed before her. She seemed genuinely grateful, conceding that she had never thought about it that way before and thanking us for allowing her to interrupt our daddy-daughter date. I assured her that she was no interruption and that engaging with her had been my honor—which it truly was.

Later that evening I thought back on the food court encounter. In a sense this sweet lady had indeed interrupted our chicken strip dinner. She had hijacked my time with my daughter.

But in another, infinitely greater sense, I'm convinced that Jesus interrupted *her* dinner. I'm quite certain she hadn't left her house, gotten into her car, driven to the mall, and made her way to the food court that night with hopes that someone would spend thirty minutes sharing the gospel with her. That hadn't been her plan at all! But by the grace of God, it had been His. She didn't hijack our time; He hijacked hers.

What a privilege it had been to witness the gospel made evident through the life of a little girl in a mall food court that evening!

The pulpit of adoption

Foster care and adoption are nothing less than giving our families to kids who need them, but they're so much more. The call to care for these kids doesn't stop with us but extends itself into our responsibility to posture ourselves as a pulpit upon which the gospel can most vividly and effectively be communicated to a curious world. We don't need to share the tragic details of our child's story, but we do get to share the good news of Jesus'. Their story is theirs to be told—when and however they may choose—but His story is His to be told, and He will make it clear when and how He wants that to happen.

While it isn't always the case that skin color and hair type differences make certain aspects of foster care obvious, it is always and irrefutably true that caring for the vulnerable by bringing them into our homes is one of the purest and most undefiled expressions of our faith this world will ever see (James 1:27). It preaches His story. Our job is to let it.

I want my daughter to grow up knowing two things: that (1) her story is special and powerful and that (2) it has been changing people's lives for a long time—long before she was aware of it. A particular mall food court encounter serves as evidence.

Opportunities, not annoyances

Foster care and adoption are personal megaphones through which we publicly tell the world what we believe about God. Embrace the questions, stares, assumptions, and seemingly offensive statements of others not as annoyances but as opportunities—as invitations to engage in the privilege and responsibility you've been given in foster care to offer the gospel message to those around you.

Questions, comments, and curiosity about foster care come with the territory when you bring a child into your home. They're an ever-present aspect of the whole experience.

While most such conversations are hugely encouraging and civil, there are those that aren't so much. Yet even in those less than helpful encounters I'm convinced that the majority of people aren't intentionally malicious or insulting (although it may come across that way at times). They may not be particularly knowledgeable, articulate, or tactful, but the truth is that they're simply wondering—trying to make sense of what they are seeing but not understanding.

There are often deeper questions, as well as concealed thoughts and concerns underlying what's actually being expressed, and it's in those moments that foster care extends beyond our care of kids into our concern for those who are wondering, asking, considering, and possibly wrestling with the meaning and implications of what they're observing or experiencing. Perhaps in those moments it's more than likely not about their interrupting whatever it is we're doing but about Jesus wanting to interrupt whatever it is they're doing.

Develop your "elevator speech"

All of this isn't to say that EVERY conversation needs to constitute a deep theological treatise on the nuances of salvation. Not at all. Sometimes short, pleasant responses before moving on are sufficient. What it does mean is that we can always be helpful, kind, and generous in our dealings with people, even if this involves no more than a thirty-second interaction with the checkout clerk at the grocery store.

Consider developing what is commonly referred to as an "elevator speech." Imagine that you're in an elevator with someone who asks you, "Why do you do foster care?" The catch is that you have about thirty seconds max before the doors open and one or the other of you gets out. What do you say? It's important for us to be prepared to answer people's questions as well as we can, in a manner that's informative, helpful, and encouraging for them. Spend some time writing out your personal "elevator speech" in response to the following questions/prompts:

- Why do you do foster care?
- Why are these children in foster care? What happened to them? (Remember that it's important to honor and protect the child's story, especially in front of the child.)
- Did the child's parents do drugs? Were they abusive? Are they in jail? (Remember that it's important to honor their parents' story too, especially in front of the child.)
- Respond to this statement: "I could never do what you do. I would get too attached."
- Respond to this statement: "This child is so lucky to have you."
- When speaking to a nonbeliever, how would you go about bringing the gospel and God's heart into the dialogue?
- If you have other children, how do you ensure that all of the attention in a social setting isn't being focused on the foster child? How do you honor your other children by making sure they aren't being consistently overlooked in public?

James 1:27

Pure and undefiled religion before God the Father is this: to care for orphans and widows in their misfortune and to keep oneself unstained by the world.

In many ways, this very familiar passage is not saying what we often think it is saying . . . but it is saying so much more! James is not commanding us to do anything; instead he is describing something very beautiful to us — or in his words, "pure and undefiled." In effect, he's suggesting that one of the purest and most undefiled outward demonstrations of what we believe about God is to care for some of the most vulnerable among us. In other words, when we move towards hard places and broken people it says something true about what God the Father has done for us.

To dive deeper into this check out "James 1:27 is Not a Command" at www.jasonjohnsonblog.com.

Like a shadow

Foster care incarnates the gospel with great vividness and clarity. Like a shadow, it allows you to bring Jesus with you wherever you go—to the grocery store, the restaurant, and even the food court at the mall. People can't help but wonder and will often stop and stare, ask questions, and/or clumsily fumble through awkward and sometimes comical interactions with you. This conversation may well be unlike any they've had before, and their attempts to put words to their scattered and unscripted thoughts may be feeble at best. Yet we have the solid answers to provide them.

The pulpit has been constructed, the audience is captive, and the privilege of pointing to Him is humbling.

Foster care preaches the gospel. It's our privilege to allow it.

" Foster care and adoption are personal megaphones through which we publicly tell the world what we believe about God.

PERSONAL REFLECTION

1. Why is it important for us to view such encounters not as annoyances but as opportunities? What is the current posture of your heart: Are you in a place of frustration over what you view as intrusions into your privacy and interruptions of your time? If so, what steps can you take to realign your perspective and attitude?

2. What comments or questions have been put to you about foster care or adoption that caught you off guard? How did you *want* to answer them? Were you able to think of a helpful and encouraging way to respond? Consider taking some time over the next few days to develop your "elevator speech" so you can be prepared with meaningful and encouraging responses to curious people.

3. How, if at all, has foster care functioned as a pulpit upon which the gospel has been preached to you?

GROUP DISCUSSION

1. What truth or idea stood out for you most strikingly in this session? Why?

2. What are some of the strangest, the most encouraging, and even the most unintentionally offensive things people have said to you about your involvement in foster care? Why is it important to perceive these encounters not as annoyances but as opportunities?

3. Why do you think people have no "category" in which to file what they're seeing or have come to understand

about your family? What is there about our willingness to open our homes to these kids that strikes people as so "different" or confusing? What causes those around us to say and ask some of the things they do?

4.   Has there been a time when your helpful response turned into a more lengthy and meaningful dialogue? How did that conversation come about? What did you learn from it? What was the outcome (if you know)? How have you found balance between the importance of protecting a child's story and your desire to share God's heart, as demonstrated through the life of this child?

PLAN OF ACTION

1.   What specific perspectives, attitudes, or ways of thinking might need to change in order for you to more effectively live out the ideas discussed in this section?

2.   What specific actions or behaviors might need to change in order for you to more meaningfully live out the ideas discussed in this section?

3.   Based on what has been discussed in this section, complete the following statement as thoroughly and honestly as you can: *I will choose to honor God through this by . . .*

God blesses his people with extravagant grace so they might extend his extravagant glory to all peoples on the earth.

DAVID PLATT

CHAPTER 17

REHUMANIZING FOSTER CARE

Foster care can be cold and sterile.

Like courtrooms, medicaid offices, or waiting rooms in doctors' offices.

The human aspect of foster care is often lost in the bureaucracy. In the bustle of training hours, paperwork, court hearings, and doctor appointments, the fact that we're dealing with real people who have real struggles and are suffering real consequences can be easily forgotten. This isn't to say that foster care is boring or monotonous—it's anything but. It is to say, however, that the places foster care takes you and the demands it makes on you can sometimes feel more legal than relational and more painstaking than life-changing.

Cases can languish on for months, if not years, while our emotions follow suit. Shock over the atrocities committed against kids can haunt us deeply and harden us to the core. Frustration with an overworked caseworker, an inexperienced lawyer, or an overrun system can numb us to the reality that all parties involved, including ourselves, are humans. Not systems. Not governments. Not bad guys or good guys. Not machines.

Just people. Broken and vulnerable people.

No one is strutting their way through foster care; we're all limping in some way, each of us wired for struggle and worthy of grace—biological parents, kids, caseworkers, lawyers, judges, and sometimes especially ourselves, the foster parents.

Nowhere is this truer than in our interactions with and attitudes toward four particular groups of people that contribute their uniquenesses and limitations to the process from beginning to end. While they're distinct in their identities and roles, these individuals share at least one commonality—they're all human. At the end of the day, they're people. And it's important for us to remember this.

Caseworkers

Child welfare caseworkers wade deeply through the bogs of brokenness, abuse, neglect, and oppression on a daily basis. They stand in court on behalf of vulnerable children and do the hard work of documenting the implications and outcomes of brokenness most of us go to great lengths to avoid. They're instructed to use their best judgment in determining whether the evidence of an investigation warrants removing children from their homes—even while assuming the possibility of a significant risk in leaving them there and hoping everything will be okay. They're then expected to sleep well at night and to function socially, emotionally, and spiritually, as though this were just another day at the office. They're overworked, overwhelmed, under-resourced, and overly criticized. They're humans expected to do a job that only a machine could effectively perform. They aren't robots—they're people. Not emotional vacuums but souls and consciences that carry a heaviness under the weight of which most of us would crumble.

It goes without saying that there are some caseworkers who prove themselves unwilling, cold, and/or utterly inadequate in terms of their ability to determine what's in the best interest of the child. Their humanity isn't an excuse for their incompetency. But we don't judge the whole on the basis of the actions of a few. Instead we empathize, humanize, and pray for their strength, wisdom, and endurance. They do difficult and too often thankless work.

Biological parents

I'll never forget the first time we sat across the table from the biological mother of the little girl who would eventually become our daughter. A few months had passed since the fragile newborn to whom this mother had given birth had been brought to our home by Child Protective Services—a period of time during which I had vilified and demonized her in my heart for what she had done to such a precious, innocent child. We now sat across the table from the very woman I had convinced myself was nothing but evil; while one part of my heart longed to hate her, I was surprised to find another part of me wanting to hug her.

Through deep sobs she shared her story of childhood abuse, chronic addiction, and long-term demons in her life she couldn't seem to shake. For the first time I realized something profoundly simple: she wasn't a demon at all—but a human. A broken one, like me. Nor was she my enemy. She was actually, somehow and in some way, my responsibility.

Her brokenness broke me, forcing me to put down the weapon held ready in my heart and instead to take a good, long look into the mirror of my soul.

It's imperative for us as foster parents to humanize biological parents, not demonize them. They're real, complex, and multi-faceted people enduring deep struggles and in desperate need of a real Savior. It is entirely possible to see biological parents as humans, not demons, yet still stand adamantly against the heinous things they have done. We can be against their actions but still for their souls. We can hate what they've done but still be FOR them. Hard, indeed, but a struggle worth wrestling with.

The kids

It was a Wednesday night, around 7:30, the first time a child was brought to our home. We watched through the front window as the caseworker parked in our driveway and walked toward the front door. Strapped into the carseat dangling from her arm was a tragically fragile little girl who needed a home to live in and a family to love her. As I've recalled earlier, this was the best and the worst day of her short life to that point—and one that would change ours forever. While pain, abuse, and brokenness had brought her to our front door, it was love and the hope of healing that welcomed her in. We celebrated the opportunity to care for her even while we ached over the reality that someone had put her in a position of needing our care in the first place.

Years later, it is now our joy to call her our daughter; it's also our great sadness that any of this ever had to happen to her. This is her real human story—one that we, in the most ideal of senses, have unfortunately had to become a part of. It's a story of deep emotions that will undoubtedly work to shape and define her in many ways for the rest of her life.

Children in foster care aren't causes; they're kids—not objects to be acquired, projects to be undertaken, or trophies to be displayed. They're real people experiencing real tragedy and in need of real help. When they become anything less than human in our eyes, we have ceased serving their best interests and have started using them as pawns to promote our own. While we certainly celebrate the opportunity to care for them, we mourn all that has been lost for them in the process.

Foster parents

Allow me to repeat that you don't have to be a perfect parent in order to be a perfect candidate for foster parenting. Inherent in the role is the pressure to *be amazing*; after all, *what you're doing truly is something amazing* (you've been told this over and over again). Trouble is, "amazing" is an absolutely unrealistic, utterly impossible expectation for any of us humans to live up to. Far from being saints, heroes, or spiritual rock stars, foster parents are precisely what the rest of us are: authentic, created—and tragically sin-marred—human beings. Real moms and dads who struggle, stumble, and get annoyed, frustrated, and depleted. Who not only don't have all the answers but often don't begin to know the questions to ask.

Give yourself some grace—God is anything but stingy in doling it out to you! Cut yourself some slack. Your job isn't that of savior—that role has been taken; your calling is simply to love these kids as representatives of the true, capital-S Savior who loved and continues to love you. God didn't call you to this because he thought you could handle it. He called *you* because He knew *He* could. He is using you, a mere human, to help resolve a seemingly insurmountable human problem. Confusion, frustration, and exhaustion are inevitable and unavoidable, but He is faithful, infinitely good, and right there with us, offering us His undivided attention even when we're curled up in the fetal position bawling our eyes out because we aren't sure we can handle any more of this.

The good news is that Jesus neither calls nor expects you to control everything—let's make that *anything!*—in the foster care process. Truth is, He wants you to be okay with the fact that you can't. Your "success" as a foster parent will be determined not by your capacity to keep everything in order but by your ability to trust that even in the chaos Jesus is beautiful—and even in the mess, what you're doing for these kids is too.

" No one is strutting their way through foster care; we're all limping in some way— each of us wired for struggle and worthy of grace.

PERSONAL REFLECTION

1. How has your engagement with the foster care system reminded you of the humanity of the other participants, in whatever their role? In what particular context are you most vulnerable to losing sight of this reality? Who is it you struggle the most to humanize?

2. In what ways do you at times find it difficult to "humanize" yourself? What steps can you take to offer yourself more grace?

3. What aspects of the gospel have become most relevant to you as you've become increasingly aware of the need to "humanize" everyone involved in the fostering process? If God Himself were seated across the table from you offering His counsel on how He wants you to relate and respond to caseworkers, birth parents, the kids, and even yourself, what do you think He would say? In what ways do your attitudes and actions need to change/improve?

GROUP DISCUSSION

1. What truth or idea stood out for you most graphically in this session? Why?

2. Why is it important to continually be reminded of the humanity of foster care? Why is it especially difficult at certain times to maintain this perspective?

3. Whom do you struggle the most to "humanize"? Why? In what ways do you at times fail to "humanize" yourself? At what specific times does this tend to be a problem?

4. How do you reconcile being "against" what birth parents may have done while still being "in their court" in terms of wanting to see them restored and healthy? What are some ways in which we can view the well-being of birth parents as a responsibility in which we share? What practical things can we do to help them become healthy and restored . . . and ultimately to see Jesus?

PLAN OF ACTION

1. What specific perspectives, attitudes, or ways of thinking might need to change in order for you to more helpfully live out the ideas discussed in this section?

2. What specific actions or behaviors might need to change in order for you to more effectively live out the ideas discussed in this section?

3. Based on what has been discussed in this section, complete the following statement as thoroughly and honestly as you can: *I will choose to honor God through this by . . .*

Grace, like water, flows to the lowest part.
PHILIP YANCEY

CHAPTER 18

THE OTHER SIDE OF FOSTER CARE

We met her for the first time in a downtown courtroom—the same place we would see her for the last time nearly one year later. And even if we are never see her again, a piece of her will always be a part of us—quite literally.

It was the first court hearing since her baby girl had been removed from her custody by Child Protective Services and placed in our care a few weeks earlier. Given the particular circumstances of the case, the judge would soon inform her that she was on track to lose her parental rights over her child. While the law was right and just that day, the emotions were raw and real. She was devastated; the demons she couldn't get out from under were deep and destructive to both her life and her baby's.

We were overwhelmed, wondering how this world could be so broken that an entire legal system had to be set up to protect children from those who seem to love them yet still harm them. Files lined the courtroom that day, each representing a case in which a child needed to be protected and a parent needed to be disciplined. Stacks of broken stories filled the room. We were there participating in just one of the many.

A whole new world

Difficult doesn't describe it—standing for the first time with the mom of the baby the state had placed in our home and we were now loving and raising as our own. Wondering what she was thinking and feeling, what her life was like that led her to that point and bothered by the fact that nothing, and no one, had been there or been capable of preventing her from being in the position she now found herself in.

Our worlds couldn't be more different. The contrast between the two was magnified that day as they collided for the first time. One of relative ease and privilege and opportunity now standing with one full of brokenness, struggle and now tragedy.

How could we live in the same world but come from two very different ones at the same time? Why was this cold, sterile courtroom the first time our worlds were ever intersecting?

These questions haunted us. Not simply because they revealed something so tragically wrong and broken about the world we live in but because they also revealed something radically wrong and broken in ourselves. The burning question wasn't so much *How come no one was there for her to help prevent this from happening?* as it was *How come we— the collective, societal, Christian, not to mention our family personally we—weren't there for her—or there to intervene in any of the other hundreds of stories represented by the files in that room?* Who was ultimately responsible? Why weren't we? How might we go about doing our part? In what kind of small, insular, and complacent world had we enveloped ourselves, allowing us to live out our daily lives oblivious to our absolute disconnect from her reality?

Two worlds collided that day, and we saw in raw, undeniable ways the extent to which all of us, at the end of the day, are part of the same world—together in this thing called life. Or at least, we should be.

The other side of foster care

Fostering abused, neglected, and vulnerable children is by nature reactionary—a necessary response to circumstances often requiring swift, immediate, and sometimes severe measures to protect the rights of the most vulnerable among us. Despite its inescapable flaws, it is overall a good, right, and just solution to a very real problem—though neither the only nor the ultimate one.

On one side of the spectrum is the need for us to respond to the plight of defenseless kids and intercede on their behalf. It's right and honorable and a reflection of the heart of God to secure and protect the rights of the helpless. On the other side of foster care is the need to proactively respond to the brokenness of families and intercede on *their* behalf to prevent their children from ever finding their way into the system. This too is right and honorable and a reflection of the heart of God to bring healing to what is broken and hope to what otherwise is headed toward destruction.

In 2012 we stood in a cold, sterile courtroom for the first time on one side of foster care; four years later we would sit in our own living room deeply entrenched in the other.

It started with a text, and then more texts, a series of phone calls, and ultimately an impromptu meeting at our house. Close friends were keeping us up to speed on an emergency situation as it unfolded. A young girl they had known for quite some time, the strong and resilient product of an extremely difficult life—we'll call her "Kay"—was now twenty-three years old. With essentially no home, no job, and virtually no support, she lay in a hospital room having just given birth to two beautiful twin girls. Child Protective Services had already begun delivering their ultimatum: find a job and a place to live or lose the babies.

The question between us and our friends that evening wasn't *Should we do something?*—that answer was clear: under no circumstances were any of us going to allow those newborns to slip into the system. It was really more a question of *how*. That was a bit more complicated. Where would Kay live? For how long? Were we crazy for even suggesting involvement in this? Could we really handle it?

The longer we discussed potential solutions, the clearer the inevitable answer became: it would come down to our two families, working in tandem to make this thing happen. Neither of us could care for Kay and her babies alone, but maybe, just maybe, if we banded together we could handle it.

And that's what we did. Kay and the babies had a room in each of our homes. A meal calendar was set up so that friends, acquaintances, and even total strangers from our church could help provide. We took turns with middle-of-the-night feedings, as well as with running Kay to various appointments and helping her get her social services set up, a new apartment secured, and a plan of action for transitioning back into her new normal on her own as a single mom of newborn twins. Some days were as sweet as rocking precious little ones to sleep in our arms. Others were quite the opposite—messy, complicated, and downright awful—the kind of hard we could have never handled on our own. But, walking this journey within the context of community, we were able to love Kay and her babies better together than either of us as couples could ever have done alone.

Kay isn't without struggles today. She continually needs the support of the community around her, a structure that was forged on her behalf in the midst of a potentially catastrophic situation. It's by no means a foregone happily-ever-after scenaro at this point, but those baby girls haven't spent one second of their young lives in foster care. That alone is a success worthy of celebration.

It was our privilege together with friends to welcome Kay and the babies into our homes for several months, give her the time she needed to adjust to life with two infants, get back on her feet, and ultimately stand on her own. Our lives are inextricably linked forever—and I'm convinced we're all better because of it.

This is the "other" side of foster care.

A joy not devoid of heartache

The new reality of our family, having adopted that little girl from foster care as our own, is that we live with the forever joy of hearing her call us Mommy and Daddy—a joy that is never fully devoid of the heartache that maybe, just maybe, all of this in an ideal world could have been avoided. The first time we met our baby girl's mom shouldn't have been in a courtroom chaperoned by lawyers and standing before a judge. Perhaps long before our worlds collided they should have intersected in a different way—perhaps in our living room, . . . or better yet, in hers. Then, maybe, just maybe, something could have been done to prevent what has happened from ever happening.

Perhaps rather than simply responding to the consequences of other peoples brokenness we have a responsibility to proactively engage them in the midst of it—to help effect healing and hope and to minimize, if not render null and void all together, repercussions perpetuating themselves any further. Church happens in those places—not just in our Sunday spaces.

In the end, perhaps the call of the Church isn't just to foster abused, neglected, and vulnerable kids but also to help prevent others like them from becoming abused, neglected, and vulnerable. Let's be at the same time the backdoor response to the need for children to be placed in permanent families and the proactive force laboring to close the front door on any new children being removed from their homes and added to the stacks of files that, I absolutely believe, shouldn't exist at all.

There's no easy solution to this; but maybe that's the point. It's not supposed to be easy. It's not a fairy-tale. It's a tragedy. One that at a minimum demands we consider the other side of. A joy not void of heartache—this is where the Church thrives.

This is the "other" side of foster care.

> **Perhaps the call of the Church isn't just to foster abused, neglected, and vulnerable kids but also to help prevent others like them from becoming abused, neglected, and vulnerable.**

PERSONAL REFLECTION

1. What is your current posture with regard to the birth families of children who are in need of help? How can you ask God to increase your capacity for compassion, not only for the child but for the family as well?

2. In what concrete ways have you experienced the "joy not devoid of heartache" in fostering? How has your ambivalence driven you to change some of your perspectives and attitudes?

3. What aspects of the gospel have been most relevant to you as you have become increasingly aware of your role and responsibility with regard to "the other side" of foster care? If God Himself were seated across the table from you offering His counsel on how He wants you to relate and respond to birth families, what do you think He would say? In what areas do your attitudes and actions need to change/improve?

GROUP DISCUSSION

1. What truth or idea sprang into focus for you in this session? Why?

2. Why is it important that we maintain clear perspectives on "the other side" of foster care? What are your thoughts on the idea of foster care being "reactive" in nature, as opposed to the more proactve prevention efforts? Do the two play an equal role in terms of moving toward

resolution? In what ways have you felt burdened for birth parents, and what have you considered doing about it?

3. What have your interactions with birth parents been like? (This is asked with the understanding that all cases are unique and not every situation affords the opportunity to personally engage with birth families.) What have you learned through them? What is your current posture toward birth parents? Fear? Anger? Disgust? Uncertainty? Compassion?

4. How would you counsel friends just getting involved with foster care on how best to prepare emotionally for the unique and the hard with regard to interraction with birth parents?

PLAN OF ACTION

1. What specific perspectives, attitudes, or ways of thinking might need to change in order for you to more responsibly live out the ideas discussed in this section?

2. What specific actions or behaviors might need to change in order for you to more effectively live out the ideas discussed in this section?

3. Based on what has been discussed in this section, complete the following statement as thoroughly and honestly as you can: *I will choose to honor God through this by . . .*

*We want to avoid suffering, death, sin, ashes. But we live in
a world crushed and broken and torn, a world God himself
visited to redeem. We receive His poured-out life,
and being allowed the high privilege of suffering with Him,
may then pour ourselves out for others.*

ELISABETH ELLIOT

STORY

I'll never forget the first phone call we shared. She was very nervous, and so was I. She had her stereotypes of folks like me, and I had mine of folks like her. But when our lives suddenly collided, everything changed.

"Hi, Sandra. I'm Jami." (*name changed for privacy)

Just a few days earlier I had been pacing the floor. I was nervous, excited, . . . and clueless about the craziness we were about to step into. When the caseworker pulled up, I ran out to the car and for the first time caught a glimpse of Dayd (three years of age) and Bobby (seven months). Oh, Dayd—he was so quiet, so scared. I picked him up and kissed him on the forehead and told him, "I'm so glad you're here."

We had walked through a journey of heartbreak that opened our eyes and hearts to children in foster care, so when God brought these kids into our home we were overjoyed. But on the other side of our joy was a family that had been ripped apart. *On the other side of our joy was a mom and dad whose arms were empty and whose hearts were broken.*

To hear Sandra's voice that day and then, gradually, over the next several months, to learn of her story, her fears, and her hopes developed in me such love for her.

Sandra herself was the product of foster care, and, sadly, like so many others in her situation, she was perpetuating the hopeless cycle for her kids.

When she became pregnant yet again, she asked me to be there with her as she gave birth. I was honored by her invitation but terrified at the same time because of my tendency to pass out in a hospital setting.

I knew that if I were going to be any sort of support to Sandra, the Lord would have to work supernaturally in me!

I'll never forget that day. The phone call came at 9:00 a.m. She was having contractions every few minutes and needed a ride to the hospital, as there was no gas in their car. I was still in my pajamas getting ready to take my kids to school. I called Clint, and he was able to pick her up and take her to the hospital.

I arrived about forty-five minutes later, and after her pain was under control she started telling me about how Clint had picked her up. He cleaned off the seat for her and made jokes about how long it had been since he'd taken a pregnant woman to the hospital. She hadn't found it very funny at the time, as she was in pain—but nevertheless, the fact that he came meant the world to her. I could see it all over her. She felt so special, so cared for, so loved.

Sitting there that day with Sandra, I thought about how important her presence had come to be in my life, and I saw firsthand how powerful mine was to her.

It was evident: there was power in just *being there*.

I sat with Sandra, breathed with her, encouraged her, and stayed by her side during her labor and delivery. She asked me to cut the baby's cord, and I held him for five minutes after he was born, sang "Jesus Loves Me" to him, and whispered prayers over his life. That day was profound—one I'll never forget.

Sandra has made mistakes, yes—big ones. But Sandra, like me, was created by God for a beautiful purpose. She is His prized possession, deserving of dignity, respect, and love.

People like Sandra don't need our judgment. *They need our presence.* They need us to step into their lives—to walk along with them and SHOW them Jesus through the way we live. They need us to believe in them, mentor them, and invest in them.

These vulnerable parents aren't the enemy. The enemy is the one who sneaks about like a roaring lion, seeking whom he can destroy. The enemy is the one who kills, steals life, and works tirelessly to destroy.

Let's step up and fight! But let's make sure we're fighting the real enemy and *be there* for those who are hurting, broken, and forgotten.

Jami Kaeb
Wife to Clint, Mom to 7 (5 through adoption),
Executive Director of The Forgotten Initiative

CHAPTER 19

CRUCIFYING THE HERO COMPLEX

If we aren't careful, our care of vulnerable kids and families can become shrouded in an evangelical hero complex that makes it more about ourselves than about them. In the end, our good works can be promoted on the backs of the vulnerable, to the detriment of Jesus being proclaimed as the true hero in all of this.

The idol of foster care

Our call to care for the orphaned and vulnerable is more about the help they need than it is about our need to help. We can't use foster care as the means by which we gain our ultimate sense of fulfillment, purpose, or meaning. Only Jesus can provide that for us.

Many of these kids experience horrendous atrocities and injustices in a very short amount of time. The last thing they need is to have us using them to mask our own insecurities by burdening them with an expectation that they satisfy our self-righteous need to help someone less fortunate. In this paradigm foster care deteriorates into an idol, or a service project—a work upon which our identity is based and our self-justifying needs are met.

These defenseless kids aren't trophies for us to put on display so people will know how obedient, radical, and missional we are. The end goal of our obedience in caring for kids in foster care isn't the display of our own obedience but the child's gain of precisely that which we're called to lose: ourselves. It's solely about what is best for them, not what is glamorous or daring or risky or evangelically sexy for us.

The rude realities

Fostering and adopting abused, neglected, and vulnerable children is a big deal, but it expresses itself primarily through very small, menial, hidden tasks that go largely unnoticed. The rude realities of foster care find us up for 3:00 a.m. feedings, changing the diaper of a baby who isn't even ours for what may seem like the hundredth time that day; on the phone with caseworkers, lawyers, doctors, or government departmental offices; filling out stacks of paperwork; sitting through court hearings; driving across the city for parent visits; and trying desperately to manage behavior born of trauma. This is a far cry from donning our superhero capes and parading our multiracial family down the hallway at church or through the aisles of the grocery store, hoping that people will notice and applaud just how awesome we are.

Yes, foster care is a big deal, but its grandness isn't measured by the public fame it produces. Rather, it's measured by the private faithfulness it requires . . . when no one is around to see, no one cares, and there's no chance of our earning a prize or being given a cape to wear because of it.

Jesus, the true hero

The hard but glorious call of the Christian life, in all arenas, is to lose ourselves in order to truly find ourselves in Jesus (Matthew 16:25). It's to humbly take up the cross of our own death every day, so that in Jesus we may find life (Luke 9:23). The beauty of the gospel is that Jesus never calls us to do anything that He hasn't first willingly, joyfully, and perfectly done for us. His call for us to lose our lives is a mere signpost pointing back to the great loss He endured on our behalf. His call for us to carry the cross is but a shadow of the death He joyfully endured in our place.

In light of the gospel, our call to care for vulnerable kids is all about the joyous privilege we have of losing ourselves for their sakes, because He first lost Himself for ours. We carry the burden of their plight because He first carried the unjust and undeserved weight of ours . . . to His death. He alone is the hero in all of this; we are but shadows. He is the hero—we are but signposts.

We don't strut into these kids' stories with a cape on our shoulders; we crawl into them with the cross on our back. Herein lies our hope: that in all of our efforts for them we are ultimately freed from any self-imposed burden of trying to make it about us. There's room in the gospel for only one hero, and it isn't going to be me or you.

So let's put down the cape and pick up the cross.

Everyone wins if Jesus is pointed to as the hero. If not, everyone loses.

> **We don't strut into these kids' stories with a cape on our shoulders; we crawl into them with the cross on our back.**

PERSONAL REFLECTION

1. In what context have you felt the temptation to operate from a "hero complex" in your fostering journey? Is this temptation more pressing when things are going well, when they're going poorly, or when you're especially busy, . . . tired, . . . or emotional?

2. What behaviors, actions, or practices have you found to be most helpful in your efforts to crucify the hero complex temptation?

3. In what ways have you seen God use foster care as an avenue upon which Jesus can be showcased as the ultimate hero?

GROUP DISCUSSION

1. What truth or idea stood out to you most clearly in this session? Why?

2. Read Matthew 16:25 and Luke 9:23 aloud together:

    "Whoever would save his life will lose it, but whoever loses his life for my sake will find it." Matthew 16:25

    "If anyone would come after me, let him deny himself and take up his cross daily and follow me." Luke 9:23

    How has foster care forced you to more fully embrace these radical calls of Jesus to discipleship and sacrifice? Be specific.

3. What behaviors, actions, or practices have you found to be most helpful in your efforts to crucify the hero complex temptation? Explain.

4. Discuss this statement as a group: "Foster care is a big deal, but its grandness isn't measured by the public fame it produces. Rather, it's divinely assessed on the basis of the private faithfulness it requires." How does this statement push against our natural human desire to be known, seen, and recognized?

PLAN OF ACTION

1. What specific perspectives, attitudes, or ways of thinking might need to change in order for you to more effectively live out the ideas discussed in this section?

2. What specific actions or behaviors might need to change in order for you to more consistently live out the ideas discussed in this section?

3. Based on what has been discussed in this section, complete the following statement as thoroughly and honestly as you can: *I will choose to honor God through this by . . .*

All heroes are shadows of Christ.

JOHN PIPER

CHAPTER 20

DIVERSITY, GUILT, AND BATTLING THE ENEMY OF COMPARISON

My brother-in-law and I live in the same town. We attend the same church, eat at the same restaurants, play on the same softball team, hang out at the same family functions, and are both relatively quiet guys. But aside from those things, we couldn't be more different.

My career has mostly involved standing on stages speaking to audiences or sitting behind computer screens writing at coffee shops. His has in large part been spent in helicopters, flying top-secret missions into parts of the world most of us have never heard of in order to train or protect us from dangers of which most of us aren't even aware. While I studied communications in my undergrad years, he went to West Point. While I went to seminary to study theology, he went to ranger school to become one of the most highly trained soldiers the United States Army has ever produced. I respect him immensely, not just because he could break my arm with his pinky finger but because he has done something I never could. And because of men and women like him, I likely will never have to.

My respect for him is, in part, rooted in my appreciation for what he has done and my gratefulness that I don't have to be the one doing it—but it cuts both ways. I know him well enough to know that he has no interest in standing on stage and preaching to an audience. He's perfectly content letting someone like me do that so that someone like him won't have to. I can celebrate the benefits of his work on my behalf, and he can appreciate the benefits of my work on his. Our work, though vastly different, is mutually beneficial.

That's the beautiful thing about diversity: we can do two entirely different things that work together for a common good.

The body of Christ in foster care and adoption

The imagery of a human body is consistently used throughout Scripture to illustrate the identity and activity of the Church—how the people of God relate to one another and function together. Some are hands and some are feet, some fingers and some toes, some eyes and some ears (1 Corinthians 12:14–20). In this diverse, interconnected system of parts, unique functions are given to unique individuals, not for their own good but for the benefit of the whole body (1 Corinthians 12:4–7).

These roles are established not on the basis of rank, as though one person's position were more important than another's, but on the premise that when each member fulfills his or her individual responsibility the whole body functions better together. Each of us does what we do so that others won't have to, and those others do what they do so that we won't have to. Distinctive roles, all serving the same purpose with equal importance: that's how our physical bodies work, and that too is how the Church most effectively operates. The point of Scripture using this imagery is this: to communicate that although we're certainly not all called to do the same thing, each of us is definitely created to do something.

If we aren't careful we may unintentionally define this work too narrowly, restricting its meaning to the context of adoption, foster care, or some other long-term form of bringing a child into our homes. While these are, of course, crucial and essential places for the Church to engage, they represent only a fraction of the limitless opportunities we have to care for vulnerable children and support the families who do. The opportunities to get involved are as unique and varied as the individual members of the body. Some will be led to foster or adopt, while others, for example, will be drawn to financially support those who do—different functions, but of equal importance.

Ask the family adopting whether they feel more important than the families helping them financially. I guarantee that they consider those supporters to be immensely important in the lives of their children, even if they aren't the ones bringing them into their home. Or ask the foster family who just took in another placement the importance of the families who bring them meals and offer to babysit. No doubt they view that support network as crucial to their ability to bring that child into their home.

Unique functions, same purposes, and all of equal importance. These, and a variety of others, are ways in which the body of Christ can work in concert to care for kids.

Identifying your something

Part of venturing down the foster care path is discovering
the unique, specific role into which God is asking you to
step, and in so doing to identify with clarity and confidence
those places to which He *isn't* leading you. I repeat: we aren't
all called to do the same thing, but each of us is capable of
contributing something. And it's essential for you to identify
your something. How do you go about doing that? Let me
suggest a few approaches:

Pray. Ask God to open your heart to Him and protect
you from the temptation to rationalize and justify—to
free you up, in other words, to just start obeying. The
goal isn't to find warm, fuzzy feelings of comfort and
peace; sometimes asking God for clarity results in His
leading us into some very hard and precarious places
that are full of uncertainty. Be willing to listen and,
most importantly, to accept whatever it is you hear
from Him. Let this be the posture of your prayer life.

Share with your community. If our unique roles
within the body of Christ were divinely given to us
for the good of the whole, then who better to ask
how we can benefit the body than its other members?
Community is a crucial filter for us in determining
where and how God is leading. If I were to go to my
friends and tell them I felt the Lord leading me away

from this ministry and into interpretive dancing ministry, I hope they would be good enough friends to tell me that I was way off in my assessment—that I had missed God big time somewhere along the line. Why? Because my attempts at performing interpretive dance wouldn't benefit the body of Christ at all! They would actually hurt it—I'm talking *really, really hurt it!* Share with your community what you're feeling and sensing. Let the other members speak into it, encourage it (or discourage it, as the case may be), and maybe even refine your vision to some degree.

Do some research. Educate yourself on the various ways there are to come alongside vulnerable kids and support the families who care for them. Read blogs, articles, and books. Attend conferences and local agency orientation classes. Talk to families in your church who are already doing something, and learn from their experiences. You'll naturally begin to find that some opportunities are clearly not for you, while others stir up a passion in your heart of which you might previously not have been aware. The point of your research isn't just awareness; it's obedience. Don't be paralyzed by all the options. Just start somewhere. It may not be the place you eventually end up, but at least you'll be out of the starting gate. That's what's important.

Battling the enemies of comparison and guilt

We've all heard amazing stories of people who have fostered fifty plus kids, adopted twelve of them, single-handedly funded an orphanage in Uganda, and run an after school program for inner city kids from their house. Okay, maybe not quite that extreme, but there are those stories that make many of us wince, step back, and think, "Wow, are you kidding me?!" It can be incredibly easy to compare what you're doing to what others have done, and just as easy to feel insignificant, inadequate, and insufficient.

Let's be clear: your "enough" isn't determined by measuring yourself against someone else; it's defined by whether you're being obedient to what God has asked *you* to do. We can't all do the same thing—nor would that be productive for the Church—but we can all find our something . . . and then go about doing it. If we were all a bunch of right feet we would run around in cirlces all day long and get nothing done. We would look busy, but ultimately be incredibly unproductive.

God will lead some people to do certain things for which you aren't equipped . . . and will likely never have to do because of people like them. And that's okay. It's how the body of Christ works. As Charles Swindoll puts it, "When the Lord makes it clear you're to follow Him in this new direction, focus fully on Him and refuse to be distracted by comparisons with others." He's right. Stop looking at what others are doing and just start doing what you're supposed to do.

Comparison to others breeds guilt in ourselves, . . . and guilt is a horrible motivator. Stop feeling guilty about what you haven't been gifted to do and start pressing into whatever it is you are. What you can do might not be the same as what others around you are doing, but that's okay too. It might mean that you say no to the next call from your caseworker, because you've reached the limits of your capacity right now in your home. It might mean that you don't sign up to take meals to the family who just welcomed a child because you're already overrun and stretched to your limit—perhaps you are in need of having meals brought to you! It might mean that you decline some opportunities, and not feel guilty about doing so, because your no may be creating an opportunity for someone else to express and explore their yes.

Fight hard against the tendency to feel as though you aren't doing *anything just because you aren't doing everything.* Let's be clear: you don't need to change the world for every child, but if what you're doing is changing the world for at least one, it's definitely significant and undoubtedly beautiful.

There's no "just" or "only" in foster care and adoption. You haven't "just" fostered a few or "only" adopted one. Rather, you have significantly altered the trajectory of a life forever. Generations to come will never be the same. There's no "just" or "only" in that. Likewise, you don't "just" bring meals to foster families or "only" babysit, donate supplies or financially support. You are participating in the renewal of all things by supporting families in the work they are doing who otherwise would not be able to do what they do without you. There's no "just" or "only" in that.

Find your something

Whatever your role, embrace it in the knowledge that in the body of Christ there are no more important or less important parts—just unique roles and players, all contributing to a whole much larger than any one individual member. The beauty of the diversity of the body of Christ as it relates to foster care is that while we're not all called to do the same thing, we are all uniquely capable of doing something.

I recently met a man in Nebraska. Mid-sixties and retired. He spends most of his time at a local equestrian center re-shoeing and caring for the horses. Many of the animals are used in equine therapy for kids who have experienced trauma, abuse, and neglect. He shared with me that while he may not be able to bring a child into his home, he can certainly take care of those horses if it means helping those kids who need them. I couldn't agree more.

I recently met a couple in Kansas City. Empty-nesters. He shared with me that he makes the best BBQ in the state (a bold claim!) and LOVES to cater any orphan-care-ministry-related event at their church, including respite nights for couples, informational meetings for those considering foster care involvement, and providing meals for families adjusting to the placement of a new child. "We know what we can't do," they conceded, "and we know what we can do, so we're going to do what we can do well." While this couple may not be in a position to bring a child into their home, they can certainly do their best to bless those who are doing so. Again, I couldn't agree more.

I recently spent time with a pastor in Oklahoma. Large, historic, traditional church. The congregation has established a significant fund in which people can invest; it's used in part to (and I quote the pastor) "ensure that under no circumstances should it cost anyone in our church one penny to foster or adopt a child." Wow! He recognizes that with a large demographic of senior adults in his body, the church has to be diligent about presenting unique opportunities that don't consist solely of bringing children into the home. There are thousands of dollars in the account right now, just waiting to be used by families engaged in foster care or adoption. Here's a church that made the same realistic assessment: "We know what we can't do, and we know what we can do, so we're going to do what we can do well." Yet again, I couldn't agree more.

I know of attorneys who donate legal services for pro bono adoptions. Mechanics who one Saturday each month offer free oil changes to single moms and foster parents. Counselors who offer their services free of charge to foster and adoptive families. The list could go on. Everyone—that's Every. One.—can do something.

The opportunities to get involved are as unique and diverse as each individual member of your church or community. Everyone has something to offer—whether it's BBQ, babysitting, a gift card, a temporary home to live in or a new forever family. While we aren't all called to do the same thing, each of us is certainly capable of doing something.

Find. Your. Something.

" While we're not all called
to do the same thing,
we are all certainly capable of
doing something.

PERSONAL REFLECTION

1. In what ways have you experienced the tendency to compare yourself to others in this fostering journey? In what context have you personally felt the guilt of comparison, of suspecting that you may not be doing enough in your fostering journey? What, specifically, has helped you (or is now helping you) move beyond that guilt?

2. In what particular ways does the gospel, demonstrated through the uniqueness of the diverse body of Christ, afford you clarity and freedom in your role—whether it be that of foster parenting, family support, or some other aspect of caring for children and families?

3. How did you identify the "something" to which God was calling you? What helped you make this determination? What role did the community around you play in your discernment of God's direction for you? How have you seen God reaffirm that calling and direction throughout your fostering journey?

GROUP DISCUSSION

1. What truth or idea stood out for you most strikingly in this session? Why?

2. As a group, read 1 Corinthians 12:4–20 together:

    Now there are varieties of gifts, but the same Spirit; and there are varieties of service, but the same Lord; and there are varieties of activities, but it is the same God who empowers them all in everyone. To each is given the manifestation of the Spirit for the common good. For to one is given through the Spirit the utterance of wisdom, and to another the utterance of knowledge according to the same Spirit, to another faith by the same Spirit, to another gifts of healing by the one Spirit, to another the working of miracles, to another prophecy, to another the ability to distinguish between spirits, to another various kinds of tongues, to another the interpretation of tongues. All these are empowered by one and the same Spirit, who apportions to each one individually as he wills.

For just as the body is one and has many members, and all the members of the body, though many, are one body, so it is with Christ. For in one Spirit we were all baptized into one body—Jews or Greeks, slaves or free—and all were made to drink of one Spirit.

For the body does not consist of one member but of many. If the foot should say, "Because I am not a hand, I do not belong to the body," that would not make it any less a part of the body. And if the ear should say, "Because I am not an eye, I do not belong to the body," that would not make it any less a part of the body. If the whole body were an eye, where would be the sense of hearing? If the whole body were an ear, where would be the sense of smell? But as it is, God arranged the members in the body, each one of them, as he chose. If all were a single member, where would the body be? As it is, there are many parts, yet one body.

What does this passage teach us about diversity coming together in unity for a common purpose? How does this picture of a physical body and the people of God living together in community uniquely apply to the fostering journey?

3. In what specific ways does the gospel give us not only the power and capacity to say yes to some things but also the freedom and confidence to say no to others? Why is it important for us to prayerfully discern when to accept and when to decline an opportunity? Why is that so hard, especially in foster care when we see so many unmet needs awaiting someone's yes?

4. How can you help initiate this "everyone can do something" culture in your church? In what specific ways can you help deconstruct false paradigms of foster care (which most people think is limited to bringing kids into our homes) and begin to expand people's understanding of the variety of ways in which they can get involved? Is there a specific person at your church with whom you can speak? An email you need to send? A meeting you need to set up to begin the conversation as it pertains to your whole church?

PLAN OF ACTION

1. What specific perspectives, attitudes, or ways of thinking might need to change in order for you to more effectively live out the ideas discussed in this section?

2. What specific actions or behaviors might need to change in order for you to better live out the ideas discussed in this section?

3. Based on what has been discussed in this section, complete the following statement as thoroughly and honestly as you can: *I will choose to honor God through this by . . .*

There is no one who is insignificant in the purpose of God.

ALISTAIR BEGG

ABOUT THE AUTHOR

Jason and his wife, Emily, became foster parents in 2012. They live in Texas with their four daughters and enjoy whatever it is they are doing, as long as it's together.

Jason is a writer and speaker who encourages families and equips churches in their foster care and adoption journeys. He also provides consulting for church and organizational leadership teams on strategic planning, messaging, resource development and effective engagement practices in the foster care, adoption, orphan care, and justice spheres.

After growing up in a ministry home in Dallas, Texas, Jason attended Texas A&M University, where he and Emily met (Whoop!). During college Jason began working at a church, and after graduating in 2002 he began his pastoral ministries studies at Dallas Theological Seminary, while engaged in full-time ministry. In 2008, alongside a core team of people in the North Houston area, Jason had the privilege of planting and leading a church within the Acts29 Network, through which he cofounded a nonprofit organization committed to serving, supporting, and equipping foster and adoptive families in the city of Houston.

In 2013, equipped with fourteen years of church-based ministry and nonprofit leadership experience, as well as his insights from his own family's foster and adoptive journey, Jason began working for an organization helping church leaders implement structures and strategies related to foster care and adoption ministry within their churches and developing resources to encourage and support families along their journeys. This ultimately led to his role as the Director of The National Church Ministry Initiative with The Christian Alliance for Orphans.

Jason speaks and teaches at churches, conferences, forums, and workshops around the country on church-based ministry strategies and best practices, and encourages families that are in the trenches and those that are considering getting involved. Much of his time is also spent coaching and consulting with church and organizational leadership teams.

Jason is the author of *Everyone Can Do Something* and *ALL IN Orphan Care* and blogs regularly at jasonjohnsonblog.com.

Here are a few different ways to connect with Jason:

- **WEBSITE:** *jasonjohnsonblog.com*
- **CONTACT:** *info@jasonjohnsonblog.com*
- **SPEAKING:** *jasonjohnsonblog.com/speakrequest*
- **FACEBOOK:** *facebook.com/jasonjohnsonblog*
- **TWITTER:** *twitter.com/_jasonjohnson*
- **INSTAGRAM:** *instagram.com/jasmjohnson*